Balancing
Mathematics
Instruction

Balancing Mathematics Instruction

Practical Ways to Effectively Implement the Math Common Core

BOOK
and DVD
Set

JAN R. CHRISTINSON

LEAD+
LEARN
PRESS

ENGLEWOOD, COLORADO

The Leadership and Learning Center
317 Inverness Way South, Suite 150
Englewood, Colorado 80112
Phone 1.866.399.6019 | Fax 303.504.9417
www.leadandlearn.com

Published by Lead + Learn Press, a division of Houghton Mifflin Harcourt.

Library of Congress Cataloging-in-Publication Data

Christinson, Jan, author.
   Balancing mathematics instruction : practical ways to effectively implement the
math common core / Jan R. Christinson.
      pages cm
   Includes bibliographical references and index.
   ISBN 978-1-935588-43-6 (Book and DVD set)
   1. Mathematics—Study and teaching—Standards—United States. I. Title.
   QA13.C47 2013
   372.7—dc23
                                                                    2013024532

ISBN 978-1-935588-43-6

Manufactured in the United States of America

 02 03 04 05 06   19 18 17 16 15 14

4500473374   A B C D E F G

I dedicate this book to Dr. Frank Klajda,
the most effective principal
that I have had the distinct pleasure of working with
and a dear friend
whose memory I will always treasure.

CONTENTS

APPENDICES

ACKNOWLEDGMENTS

I would like to sincerely thank Pam Stetka and Amanda Gomez of the Tempe Elementary School District, Sharon Daxton-Vorce and Anita Burns of the East Central BOCES, Katie Schellhorn Stoddard, whose persistence allowed this project to happen, the school administrators of Tempe, Burlington, and Byers school districts, and, especially, all the dedicated teachers and students that were filmed working in their classrooms.

A special thanks to Kevin Skattum and Anne Banister of the Light Group in Broomfield, Colorado, for their unwavering support and encouragement in the creation of the film that shows implementation in action.

And, on a personal note, I want to thank my beautiful wife, Melissa, whose love and support makes it possible for me to follow my passion.

PREFACE

Balancing Mathematics Instruction is about implementation and the practical steps that have to be taken to bring about effective change in math instruction at the classroom level to prepare students for the increased expectations of the Common Core State Standards. It is based on the insight and perspective gained about effective math instruction from more than 30 years of teaching at various levels and more than 10 years of consulting with wonderful educators across the United States.

Improving math instruction is not an easy task. With the recent acceptance of the Common Core State Standards and the current information about how students learn mathematics, this is an opportune time to change instructional practices that have not been effective for a large portion of our country's student population.

The classroom practices explained in *Balancing Mathematics Instruction* have been field-tested and refined in my classroom and in the classrooms of math teachers in various regions of the country. Dedicated math teachers have used these strategies to improve student performance in mathematics, and most importantly, to improve students' belief in their own efficacy and their attitude toward the subject of mathematics, which offers so many opportunities for students.

An underlying theme is that math instruction needs to be much more student centered to meet the expectations of the Common Core. Listening to and honoring student thinking and student ideas are critical components of effective instruction, allowing teachers to determine student misconceptions and the impact of their own instruction on student understanding.

My own classroom experience and my continued work with students and teachers in districts across the country constantly reinforces the idea that all students can not only understand mathematics and learn to effectively apply the mathematics that they are learning, but also actually see a use for the ideas and concepts contained in the subject of mathematics.

Balancing Mathematics Instruction provides practical solutions to help ensure a successful journey to improve math instruction.

JAN CHRISTINSON
Oceanside, CA

INTRODUCTION

Five Easy Steps to a Balanced Math Program (Ainsworth and Christinson, 2000) provides a useful, straightforward framework for effective mathematics instruction. *Balancing Mathematics Instruction: Practical Ways to Effectively Implement the Math Common Core* takes that concept further by explaining in detail how to implement the instructional strategies with fidelity. Based on years of experience, this book explains in a very practical way how to put these strategies in place and how to effectively implement the entire *Five Easy Steps* model.

Designed as a resource for math educators, this book can be used in a number of ways:

Supplement to workshop: Those who have attended a *Five Easy Steps to a Balanced Math Program* seminar through The Leadership and Learning Center will find that this book is an effective resource. It provides all the necessary details to effectively implement the ideas and instructional strategies that are presented in the seminar, and provides information that will enhance the overall impact of this balanced model.

Resource for districts or individual schools implementing all or portions of the *Five Easy Steps* model: This book provides the necessary resources to allow a math leadership group within a district to become more independent in terms of implementation of trained strategies. It also provides information that will help educators maintain fidelity to processes, allowing key components of the model to remain intact.

Resource for schools or districts that need effective strategies to change math instruction in preparation for the Common Core State Standards: The instructional practices promoted in each part of the balanced model automatically impact the classroom environment, creating a more student-centered process that moves math instruction toward the expectations of the Common Core State Standards in math and toward what is known about how students learn mathematics effectively. This approach makes the gradual process seem possible to teachers, and creates an atmosphere of hope and belief in efficacy for students.

Method to balance an existing math program: The implementation ideas and the strategies presented in this book will work with any commercially produced mathematics program and are meant as a model to make sure that students always receive the necessary instructional and environmental components to become proficient mathematically. School districts typically find that the use of a given textbook series produces results that show a deficit in student learning in computational strength, number sense, problem solving, or conceptual understanding, or in all four areas. The balanced model provides a structure for instruction that includes definite methods for teachers to implement while using the math standards as their guide and the textbook series as a resource. Teachers develop a balanced approach to instruction that helps to prevent students' misconceptions and gaps in their learning as they progress through the grades.

Resource for math coaches: Each section of *Balancing Mathematics Instruction*, along with the provided DVD, is an excellent resource for math coaches leading implementation of the balanced math model. The "nuts and bolts" of each process, such as "math review" and "problem solving," are provided, and film clips of students and teachers using the processes are included on the DVD.

A stand-alone resource for educators: The material and strategies in this book can be used effectively to improve math instruction for students even by those who have never attended a *Five Easy Steps* seminar or who have never even heard of *Five Easy Steps*, or the balanced mathematics model, or Jan Christinson, or The Leadership and Learning Center. All the ideas are thoroughly explained and demonstrated on the DVD. These ideas originated from my classroom, are grounded in learning theory, and have produced positive results in student learning in mathematics all over the United States in all kinds of educational environments.

Components of the Balanced Approach

In *Adding It Up: Helping Children Learn Mathematics* (2001) by the National Research Council, which is an important document in the development of the Common Core State Standards for Mathematics, the authors say that they believe "mathematical proficiency" is necessary for students to learn mathematics successfully, and that it has five components: conceptual understanding, procedural fluency, strategic competence, adaptive reasoning, and productive disposition. The idea of balance that I have been using in my classroom instruction and that will be discussed in this book matches the essence of that definition of mathematical proficiency. The "balanced approach to instruction" from the *Five Easy Steps to a Balanced Math Program* model includes development of computational strength, including number sense, application of the mathematics being learned, and understanding of the mathematics being taught.

The components of the balanced approach are:

Step 1: Computational skills—math review and mental math

Step 2: Problem solving

Step 3: Conceptual understanding—unit design

Step 4: Math fact mastery

Step 5: Common formative assessment

Inside *Balancing Mathematics Instruction*

The *Balancing Mathematics Instruction* package includes:

• Instructional strategies that will be completely explained

• Instructional strategies that will kick off the necessary change process upon implementation

• A DVD that shows filmed segments of the strategies in classrooms at various grade levels

• Practical, proven strategies that increase student proficiency and belief in efficacy in mathematics

• Discussion about the connection of each strategy to the Common Core State Standards and to good instructional practice

• Resources to help with the implementation process

The Case for Change

As a former classroom teacher and now as an educational consultant, I have observed that math education in the United States is not in very good shape, and, more importantly, that our students aren't doing well mathematically. There is a definite need for change in instructional practices to meet the expectations of the Common Core State Standards, but even more basic than that, there is a need to inspire in students the desire to pursue mathematics, and to give them reasons to seek understanding of the subject.

Our instructional methods in mathematics are not working for too many kids. Students are moving from grade to grade carrying misconceptions about concepts that accumulate to the point of complete confusion, which often causes those students to give up. It's become culturally acceptable to say at that point of confusion, "I'm not a math person." Somewhere along the line in this nation we decided that math is genetic or intrinsic, and that you can determine if a person is a "math person" or not. But most of the world believes that all students and adults are capable of learning mathematics with a competent teacher and sufficient effort. Harold Stevenson and James Stigler, in their discussion of effort and ability in math education in *The Learning Gap* (1992), conclude that "ability models subvert learning through the effects they have on the goals that parents and teachers set for children and on children's motivation to work hard to achieve these goals" (p. 106). The countries with top ratings in the 2011 *Trends in International Mathematics and Science Study* (National Center for Education Statistics)—Singapore, Korea, Chinese Taipei, and Japan—all believe in the effort model for math education. Our genetic model is problematic because it leads educators and parents to have low expectations of certain students and to label students, and it has a negative impact on students' belief in their efficacy in math. It also leads many students who might excel in math to choose not to pursue the subject. This, in the end, limits their career opportunities tremendously.

The United States has also been plagued for decades by two traditional approaches that still seem to be very prominent in every part of the country to which I have traveled in my work with schools. First, math is being taught as a set of procedures to get answers, without ensuring student understanding of those procedures. Second, material is being covered to prepare for a test or to meet a pacing guide, without concern for student understanding. There are many reasons for these two approaches, but unfortunately these teaching methods don't match what we know about how people learn, and definitely don't match what we know about how the brain functions. John Medina, in *Brain Rules* (2008), suggests that the human brain will not function efficiently in a learning mode if there is no understanding attached to what is being presented. The procedural approach may generate answers, but it is not creating understanding. An article in the *Journal for Research in Mathematics Education* (Rasmussen, et al., 2011) stated "the percentage of students needing to take remedial mathematics courses in college is on the rise" (p. 207). Further along in the article, the research committee concluded that "the focus needed to be on changing what happens in the typical high school classroom where students are not engaged, often forget important mathematical concepts from one year to the next, and are neither prepared for collegiate mathematics nor for the mathematical demands they will encounter upon entering the work force" (p. 209).

From a practical standpoint, we need to turn things around. We need student success, renewed student belief in their efficacy in math, changes in teacher practices, changes in classroom environments, and an overall change in our attitude toward mathematics. These changes will not be easy, but *Balancing Mathematics Instruction* offers guidance that will help make the journey to improved math instruction nonthreatening and exciting.

The following statements, which are based on education research and on my own experience as a teacher and as a consultant, are the foundational beliefs upon which *Balancing Mathematics Instruction* is built:

- All students can learn mathematics, including special needs students and English language learners.

- Teacher expectations and students' belief in their own efficacy are very powerful in the learning process.

- The strategies introduced here, when implemented with fidelity, can facilitate the change in instructional practice that is necessary to improve student success.

- Mathematics has to always make sense to students.

- To be more effective, teachers have to become more student centered and must diagnose the impact of their instruction by listening to students.

- The classroom should have equal amounts of student voice and teacher voice.

- Students must be engaged by a subject to learn it.

- Intellectual curiosity is fundamental to learning mathematics.

- The human brain cannot learn efficiently in situations that have no meaning or relevance.

CHAPTER 1

Math Review and Mental Math

Number Sense

Before entering into a discussion of the math review process, it's important to discuss number sense development. The Common Core State Standards emphasize number sense development in kindergarten through second grade. Basic math fact fluency, which is expected by third grade, is directly impacted by student development of number sense. Both the Common Core and the balanced approach strategies that will be described in the following chapters require that educators understand number sense development in young students and are confident in their ability to teach number sense. In the math review process, teacher understanding of student misconceptions and the error analysis process will be greatly enhanced by a thorough knowledge of number sense.

Number sense is a rather complex idea. Jessica Shumway, in her book *Number Sense Routines* (2011), says that students who have number sense "typically demonstrate these understandings and skills" (p. 10):

- A sense of what numbers mean

- An ability to look at the world in terms of quantity and numbers

- An ability to make comparisons among quantities

- Flexibility, automaticity, and fluidity with numbers

- An ability to perform mental math

- Flexibility with problems

- Automatic use of math information

- An ability to determine reasonableness of an answer

- An ability to decide on a strategy based on the numbers in a problem

Resources for Number Sense Development

- *Number Sense Routines: Building Numerical Literacy Every Day* in Grades K–3 (2011) by Jessica F. Shumway
- *Elementary and Middle School Mathematics: Teaching Developmentally* (2010) by John A. Van de Walle, Karen S. Karp, and Jennifer M. Bay-Williams
- *Teaching Student-Centered Mathematics: Grades K–3* (2005a) by John A. Van de Walle and LouAnn H. Lovin

Math Review

Math review is a structured process to help students deal with misconceptions that they have developed in their journey to learn mathematics. The process involves students doing three problems from predetermined categories within a 15-minute time frame. Students work on the same categories on a daily basis until data from the math review quiz indicates that it is time to change a category. In other words, the math review process allows students sufficient practice with a misconception to actually undo the misconception.

A math review process is essential for the success of students in our current climate of math instruction in schools. So many students are moving from grade level to grade level with misconceptions, which has devastating consequences when those students move into secondary math classes. The typical scenario is that as the grade level increases, the number of students not proficient in mathematics increases. Something has to be done, and math review is the "something" that has already helped many districts stop the flood of students who decide they can't do mathematics, and the flood of students not finding any success with mathematics. One of the major purposes and benefits of a process that is designed to correct student misunderstandings is that it keeps hope and belief in efficacy alive in the mathematics classroom.

The math review process described here originated in my classroom practice and has been refined over more than 25 years. The driving force behind what makes this student-based process work is an understanding of how people learn and of how to rectify a situation where learning has become a struggle or has become frustrating. Essential components of the math review process include repeated reasoning, effective feedback, and relational thinking.

Repeated reasoning: When students are learning a new concept or skill, or they are working on something in mathematics that has become frustrating, it is critical to their success that they have multiple opportunities to practice. In *Classroom Instruction that Works* (2012), Robert Marzano and his colleagues said they found it was necessary to have "24 attempts to reach 80 percent accuracy" (Marzano, Pickering, and Pollock, 2012, p. 111). In other words, when people are learning they need lots of chances to practice what they are learning. In the math review process, multiple opportunities to practice a given skill or concept are built into the structure.

Effective feedback: Effective feedback is specific and timely and is directly tied to the multiple chances to practice what is being learned mentioned above. In mathematics, the traditional form of feedback has been to focus on the answer. But the answer won't be sufficient feedback for students who are working hard to undo a misconception that they developed around a specific skill or concept. In the math review process, the feedback is given in a form that allows students to find out specifically which part of the problem they understand and which part or parts they are struggling with. This type of specific feedback allows students to realize that they *do* know some mathematics, and they only need to work on a piece of a particular skill. This is a big improvement over the typical feeling of struggling students who think they can't do an entire subject called mathematics ("I suck at math").

Relational thinking: Relational thinking is specific to mathematics. In general, the approach to teaching math in the United States for decades has been to take it apart into isolated skills and teach procedures to get answers. The result of this approach for students is that the meaning of the subject has been lost. Relational thinking is an idea that is fundamental to the balanced math approach. Mathematics is a subject of interconnected concepts and ideas, and through relational thinking, the meaning of mathematics becomes more and more apparent to students. Within the math review process, a focus on relational thinking is achieved by emphasizing students' ability to determine the reasonableness of an answer, their number sense, their sense of pattern, and foremost, that the math students are doing should make sense. When relational thinking is emphasized, math education does not rely on teaching tricks and sayings to help students remember how to get answers. Instead, students are given the necessary feedback for a mathematical idea to make sense to them, and for them to see the utility of that idea in other contexts.

The structure of the math review process allows students to have multiple opportunities to practice, coupled with the effective feedback that is necessary for learning, in an environment that emphasizes that mathematics makes sense. Such a classroom environment is characterized by on-task student conversation, valuing mistakes as a way to learn, teacher diagnosis of student misconception, and a belief that all students can learn mathematics.

Math Review Categories

The categories for math review are developed using several criteria. The first and most important thing to consider is what students should know mathematically when they enter the next grade level, but typically don't know. The next step in the process is to look at the priority concepts (Power Standards or Priority Standards, as described by Larry Ainsworth, 2003) for the grade that the students are entering. Other factors that can influence math review categories are Priority Standards set by state test developers, benchmark testing at the district level, and lack of student background and general knowledge.

The overall idea of developing the categories is to systematically make sure that students don't continue on with their current misconceptions and gaps in mathematics and that they are prepared to move on to the next grade level with the priority concepts mastered.

Developing the categories is a collaborative process that utilizes the experience of grade-level teachers. Described below is an activity that I have found to be effective to develop grade-level math review categories.

Category Development Process

This very informative district-level activity utilizes grade-level teacher representatives. It's best to have two or three teachers who teach math for each grade level or course. The first step of the activity is for each grade-level group or course group of teachers, using their experience, to list the concepts or skills that students should know coming into their grade level or course, but typically don't know.

The next step is for the grade-level or course groups to examine the expectations presented in their state standards (often the Common Core State Standards) and use this information to develop a list of key concepts and skills that they feel are vital to success in their grade or course. Each teacher group then discusses and finalizes each portion of the list. Upon finalization, each portion of the list is put into a sequence. In other words, *concepts and skills students should know, but don't* are listed and sequenced at the top of the list, and the *concepts and skills that are vital to success* are listed and sequenced at the bottom of the list. The final step of this portion of the activity is for each group to copy their final sequenced lists onto a piece of poster paper in preparation for the second portion of the activity.

The second portion of the activity brings the category development process for math review into the important realm of vertical alignment and grade-level articulation focused on how mathematical ideas are developed across grade levels. The Common Core State Standards documents refer to this as a "learning progression." To begin the activity, each grade-level or course group puts the poster they created on the wall in grade-level order. Each group of educators gathers around their respective poster and checks the alignment of their developed categories: Look at the poster below your grade level or course. Does your list of *concepts and skills students should know, but don't* match up with the *concepts and skills that are vital to success* from the list below your grade level? Then look at the poster above your grade level. Discuss what the next grade-level poster lists as *concepts and skills students should know, but don't.*

After the group has completed these items of discussion, each group decides if any revision is necessary for their math review category list.

Now that the category lists are finalized, the vertical alignment discussion and awareness process can begin. This process is initiated by identifying an end product for the math curriculum for the district. What is the level that is expected that all students will reach in their math careers within the district? Typically, the end product selected is either algebra I or algebra II. Having decided on an end product, the grade-level groups will now select one category on their list, then look at each poster that is below their grade level all the way to kindergarten. As the teachers are looking at the lists below their grade level, they need to ask, "Is the category we selected to look at supported and developed by the category lists of the grade levels below our grade level?" They should try this process with two or three categories, discuss their findings, and be prepared to share their conclusions.

The other point for each group to talk about is, "what conclusions can be drawn by looking at all the lists from kindergarten to algebra II?" This discussion typically leads to the realization of why a math review process is necessary, because teachers will see the same categories listed grade level after grade level, indicating that student misconceptions are not being taken care of at any grade level and students are moving on, accumulating more and more misconceptions.

The category development process activity is easily modified for use at the school level. The adjustment that has to be made is to use the last grade at the school as the agreed-upon end product. For example, an elementary K–5 school would use fifth-grade standards as the end product for the process. Category development can also be done at the individual grade level, but it won't involve the vertical alignment discussion portion, and also won't allow for any process to verify selection of categories.

The category development process improves over time, especially as teachers become more attuned to student misconceptions and more adept at diagnosing student understanding from the students' mathematical discourse.

Sample key ideas for math review categories are available in Appendix A.

Pre-Assessment Option

An interesting option for category development is being experimented with in eastern Colorado with 21 rural school districts that are supported by the East Central Board of Cooperative Educational Services (BOCES). A balanced approach to mathematics instruction is being implemented through the use of a leadership team and a curriculum team that includes representation from the districts in the region (this process is described in detail in Chapter 6).

During the first year of math review implementation, the process described above was followed to develop math review categories for the districts in the region. During the second year, the group of districts decided to develop what we called grade-level math review survey tests that would be used as an additional tool to help teachers decide the categories for their specific population within their district, school, or classroom.

The survey tests were developed by teachers who were members of the leadership team or curriculum team. The grade-level survey tests assessed the expectations for student mastery by the end of their current grade level. This process allowed teachers to give the survey test from the previous grade at the beginning of the year and use the results to determine math review categories for the section *what students should know, but don't.*

The survey tests also created consistency across the East Central BOCES region and provided a means to collect data on how math review was impacting student performance. The survey tests have recently been aligned to the Common Core State Standards.

Student Training for Math Review

The math review process is very structured and student centered, but the efficiency of the process is very dependent upon student training of certain components. What most teachers who implement math review find is that the student training that is necessary for the process is actually beneficial to their overall classroom management and their classroom's learning environment. Following are typical topics that require student training.

Paper Format

It's important to decide how you want student papers to be structured. Where will the student's name and the date go? Where will the title go? How will the students place the problems on the paper and how will they show their work? Will they need help with leaving enough space? Once the paper format is established, it is best not to change it in the math review process, because you are attempting to create student efficiency with the process so they can concentrate on the mathematics. Consistency with expectation of format will help that efficiency develop.

Showing Evidence of Solution

In the math review process, it is essential to train students to show the work that they did to solve a given problem. Math review focuses on helping students with their misconceptions and giving them the necessary feedback to undo those misconceptions. If there is no evidence of how students reached a solution, it is impossible to help them with their misconceptions, but more importantly it doesn't allow the students to participate in the structured error analysis feedback process that is the basis of the effectiveness of math review. Students need a clear and concise model of what is expected in terms of work for a given category or type of problem. Many students have never been shown how to display their work for a math problem. It is important for teachers to think through exactly how they would like the evidence of solution to be displayed on student papers, so that students can learn to meet that expectation. It's also important for students to develop the habit of showing evidence of their thought processes so that when they move toward the idea of verification of their solution, they will have a record of the steps that they followed that they are able to interpret. In the math review process, it cannot be acceptable that the answer "just popped into my head" or "I just know it." That type of response is of no benefit to the teacher or the student.

On-Task Conversations

On-task conversation training will actually help all other parts of your math instruction in addition to math review. Teachers need to define exactly what "on-task conversation" means in their classroom environment. Then students need to practice having on-task conversations several times before starting the math review process. The final step (and the ongoing step) of the training is to enforce on-task conversations during math review strictly. The benefit of the conversations is tremendous in terms of discovering student misconceptions and the reasons for those misconceptions. An effective, positive method to enforce on-task conversations is to honor student thinking as often as possible and actually celebrate with the class great conversations that you heard. The benefit to the students is that they get to practice their metacognitive skills, become better listeners, and become polite within your classroom environment.

Mathematical Discourse

The procedural approach to teaching mathematics in the United States, coupled with the overemphasis on answers and speed, has created a very interesting situation that arises when you ask students to have a mathematical conversation about solving problems during math review. Almost everywhere I travel to work with school districts, this is the typical scenario that students follow: They work the problem independently, then share their solutions. If their answers match, they say, "Yep, got the same answer, we're set"—end of conversation. If their answers are different, one of the students may say, "I'll show you what to do" or perhaps they both just sit back and say, "We'll wait until the problems are processed to find out who's right." Again, very little, if any, conversation occurs between the students.

So here is a way to help students with the idea of mathematical discourse: present the students with a script or sentence starters of what they need to say within a math conversation about working the math review problems. Recently, San Juan Unified School District in northern California has started experimenting with this idea, and an innovative teacher in Tempe Elementary School District, Katie Garcia, has been using the idea of conversation starters with first graders for two years. Basically, the idea is to structure the conversation so that students do the problems together and discuss what their first steps are, what their next steps are, and then discuss how they know that their collective solution is correct. This will automatically lead them to the idea of verification of solution and a higher level of reasoning, especially when compared to just sharing an answer and then stopping the conversation.

Math Review Partners

Math review is a collaborative process that requires that students be set up in partnerships. Partners can be established randomly for math review with a couple of exceptions. If any students are not getting along with their current partners, it is best to make a change. And if any students have been struggling on the math review quizzes, it is helpful to assign partners to those students who have shown a tendency to be helpful and kind. It is essential that on each day of math review, students know exactly who they are to work with.

Student partners should be left together for at least two weeks. A longer period of time is preferable, so that students can truly develop a collaborative relationship. Constantly switching student partners is not beneficial to this process.

Math Review Timing

Math review is designed to take, at most, 15 minutes of class time, and can be teacher directed or student directed.

Teacher directed: Students begin working the math review problems for two minutes independently, then finish working the problems for six minutes with their designated partners. The remainder of the 15 minutes is used to complete the process, which includes error analysis, reflection, and key statements.

Student directed: Students work the problems with their partner for eight minutes.

It is a good idea to use a timer that is visible to students to help the efficiency of timing for each method. Students typically don't have much experience with elapsed time and given tasks, so it is good experience for students to have feedback in the form of a timer to see how efficiently their partnership works. Students usually get increasingly efficient with this approach.

Recommendations for Student Papers

The following suggestions for student math review papers are based on what I've seen in districts across the United States that are implementing the math review process.

Kindergarten

- Manipulatives to build models of solutions
- Small whiteboards to record answers and display the answers to the teacher
- Template to record answers near the end of the school year

First Grade

- Template with problems included
- Composition booklet
- Template with problems not included

Second Grade

- Template with problems included
- Template with problems not included
- Spiral notebook/composition booklet

Third Grade to High School

- A spiral notebook is the most common form used by teachers implementing math review. Individual notebook paper can also be used and collected each day, but the papers would need to be returned each day and the students would need to keep the papers in a three-ring binder.

- The main criterion to determine the paper format for math review is that students need access to the prior day's work so they can examine the error analysis and look back at their reflections to inform their current performance with the problems. It also allows the students to have access to the key statements for the categories, which creates efficiency within the process of math review and saves instructional time.

Key Components of the Math Review Process

Student Collaboration

The math review process is dependent upon student conversation and a classroom environment that values students' explanations of their understanding. These elements are necessary to enable teachers to be able to diagnose student misconceptions.

If the classroom environment remains focused on teacher explanation, it becomes almost impossible to determine why students are struggling with a given concept or skill or how the students are interpreting the teacher's explanation through their lens of misunderstanding.

During the work session portion of math review, the teacher can quickly gather formative information about the problems in the categories by listening to students' collaborative conversations as they work the problems with their partners. If possible, it is best to form student pairs for math review. As mentioned previously, students must be trained in collaboration and on-task conversation so that they understand the expectations of the classroom teacher and can work effectively and efficiently.

Key Idea Statements

Key idea statements are important to the math review process so that teachers and students focus on the understanding that is essential to do well with a concept or skill instead of focusing on a set of steps or tricks that don't have any meaning attached.

The strategy of using key idea statements is not easy to implement because it is asking teachers and students to think differently, but the payoff is well worth the angst. Key idea statements originate from student misconceptions and from the teacher listening to student conversations pertaining to a given concept or skill. Key idea statements are not lists of steps, and are definitely not sayings or tricks (e.g., "Don't wonder why, just invert and multiply").

Key idea statements are statements of the understanding that the teacher wants the students to have concerning a given problem. The process of developing these statements is difficult at first, but then improves rapidly as the mindset of teachers changes to meaning-based statements and as teachers become more diagnostic and student centered in their approach to instruction in general and to math review in particular.

An interesting device called knowledge package can be useful in the process of developing key idea statements. The knowledge package process will be fully explained in Chapter 3.

Error Analysis

Error analysis is essential to math review. This is the part of the process where students receive the timely and specific feedback that is so important to the learning process, especially if it is attached to learning that has been frustrating and quite defeating to students. Also, error analysis gives students the opportunity to fix their mistakes immediately upon receiving feedback.

Error analysis in math review provides the necessary feedback to students about a given problem to let them know specifically what parts of the problem they are doing correctly and what parts of the problem are still giving them trouble. Error analysis within the math review process involves showing each specific part of the solution to the problem and having the students indicate how they did on each portion of the solution.

The challenge for the teacher is to decide what needs to be emphasized in any given problem. Error analysis needs to be planned out based on student misconceptions. Teachers also need to consider learning progressions within the Common Core State Standards and in general how a given concept is learned over several grade levels. Error analysis implementation improves with continued use of math review. The second year of error analysis implementation is typically much improved over the first year of implementation.

Here are some questions for teachers to use to plan out the error analysis for a problem in math review:

- Why is the problem included in math review?

- What student misconception is connected to the problem?

- What part of the problem will need to be highlighted in error analysis?

- What is the essential understanding needed for student proficiency?

- Are the key idea statements and the error analysis directly connected?

Examples of error analysis are available on the DVD included with this book.

Student Reflection

Student reflection is essential to the math review process, but it is the component that is most often left out when the math review process is implemented. Unfortunately, student reflection is typically left out of the learning process, but it is a very important feedback step on the journey to proficiency.

Reflection allows the brain to digest feedback received about a recent performance. If reflection is not facilitated, the feedback is essentially wasted. In the math review process, reflection is of the utmost importance, and is typically valued by students, but many teachers don't see the value of reflection, and it therefore gets left out of the process. Reflection in math review needs to be specific to the error analysis, and should include math vocabulary that matches the problem that is being worked on. The reflection should basically summarize what happened in the error analysis. If the students were lucky enough to correctly complete all parts of a given problem, then they will be stating exactly what they know mathematically. If they had to fix part of a problem, they will be stating specifically what they need to work on mathematically. Student reflections should be complete sentences that reflect what happened in the error analysis. They should not contain general statements about being awesome at math or being lousy at math.

It takes time to help students develop the capacity to write specific reflections about their mathematical ability, so teachers will have to be patient and facilitate the process through modeling. Teachers should have students share reflections verbally and then listen for good examples of specific reflections. Have those students share their reflections with the class as models of what is expected. Over time, student reflections will improve.

Students typically like the reflective process, but keep in mind that they may never have experienced reflective processes before, and therefore might initially need help with it. One method to build student capacity with reflection is to have students nominate other students' reflections as good examples to be shared with the class. This is an effective means by which students can honor each others' work, and it also lets the teacher know if students are increasing their overall understanding of what makes an effective reflection within the math review process.

The goal is to have student reflections match their error analysis on a daily basis to facilitate the improvement process.

Processing Math Review Problems

Teacher-Directed Method

The teacher-directed method of processing math review problems is of the utmost importance. It sets the expectations for the problems in terms of what work needs to be shown by students, what the error analysis will emphasize within the problem, and what the key idea statement is. The sequence for this method is described in the form of a script in the following section. Classroom examples can be viewed on the DVD that is included with this book.

Student-Directed Method

The student-directed method involves students directly in the processing portion of math review. It also helps create the necessary student-centered environment that enhances the overall process and significantly increases student engagement. In the student-directed method, students will basically be doing what the teacher does in the teacher-directed method. A major difference between the two methods is that the student-directed method is an agree/disagree process. This means that when students present their solutions step by step, they will be asking the other students in the class if they agree or disagree during the error analysis portion of the process.

A script for this method is included in the following section. Examples of the method can be viewed on the DVD included with this book.

Group Answer Method

This optional method is lots of fun, engaging, and very useful the day before the math review quiz. It might take a little more time than the normal math review sequence, but I have found that the benefits to students make it worthwhile. The overall idea is to involve as many students as possible in a student-directed approach. Students benefit from doing the group answer the day before the math review quiz because it enables them to find out exactly what they need to practice for the quiz.

The sequence of the group answer method, for a class of 24 students, is as follows:

- Place students in groups of four. (Have each student number off from one to four.)

- Tell the students that at the end of the eight-minute work time, a number from one to four will be randomly selected, and the person from each group that has the selected number will be part of the processing of the problems. The catch is that even when the students are selected, they won't know which problem they have to explain until the teacher assigns them a problem.

- The groups of four will do the math review problems together in sequence during the typical eight-minute work time provided in math review. Doing the problems together means that all students go through the problem step by step, and they make sure that all agree with the steps and understand the steps. Then the students in the group make sure that all four of them know why the answer is correct, because they do not know who in the group will be called upon to explain the answer. When all members of the group are finished with problem number one, then the group moves on to problem number two and follows the same procedure as they did for problem number one. The students know that any one of them may be selected to process one of the problems in front of the class, so part of the benefit of this method is that students check with each other to make sure everyone understands before moving on to the next problem.

- At the end of the eight-minute work time, the teacher randomly selects a number from one to four. The students with that number come to the front of the room with their math review papers. The teacher randomly assigns two students to each problem and gives them a couple of minutes to prepare for the processing of their assigned problem.

- At this point, the student presenters follow the regular student-directed sequence using the agree/disagree process as they present the problem.

- Student reflections can be modified so that they become a study guide for the math review quiz. The students can write down what they need to practice specifically for each problem so that they can do well on the assessment the following day.

Pass the Pen Method

The pass the pen method can be used occasionally to enhance student engagement during math review or can be used during the initial training stage to help reluctant students become more involved. It works best with problems that have a sequence that can be followed to reach a solution.

The pass the pen process is very simple: The teacher selects a student to do the first step of solving the problem, and hands the student a whiteboard marker or whatever tool is being used to record the steps for the class. The student then shows the first step to the class and does the agree/disagree procedure. Then the student selects another student to hand the "pen" to. This student will do the next step of the solution. This sequence is followed until the entire problem is processed, including the reflection and key idea statement. The teacher can set up rules for passing the pen, such as to select someone from another group, or alternate between boys and girls. Of course, the teacher will also need to set up behavior rules about the pen so you don't end up with pens flying through the air in the classroom.

This is a very risk-free method if you allow kids to say "no" to the pen if they are very unsure. Some teachers who have used this method have told students they can say no to the pen one time a week.

Script for the Teacher-Directed Method

To ensure that key components are included, follow this sequence:

1. Students indicate designated partner.

2. Students write their name, the date, and the title "Math Review" on their papers.

3. Students work on the math review problems for two minutes independently, getting as much finished as they can, but completion is not expected during this time frame.

4. Students work with their designated partner for six minutes to complete the math review problems.

5. At the end of eight minutes, students stop working on the math review problems, put away their pencils, and hold up their marking pens. It's OK if students are not finished with the problems.

Following Directions

6. Say the following to students to reinforce following the directions that have been established: "Put a star beside your name. Also star the date. Star the title 'Math Review'. Check your partner's paper to see if those elements are in place. Say to your partner, 'You are good at following directions' or 'You need to follow directions.' Check to see if you numbered your problems, copied the problems on your paper, and showed all of your work. If you did, write 'I'm awesome at following directions' on your paper. If you didn't do all those things, write 'I need to follow directions' on your paper."

Processing

Offer specific feedback for each problem in the form of error analysis, student reflection based on the error analysis, and writing and saying the key idea statement for each problem.

7. Say to the students: "Star the vocabulary word for the problem if you wrote it on your paper. If you didn't write it, you can write the vocabulary word on your paper now."

Error Analysis

8. Say to the students: "Star the first part of the problem if you have it correct. If you don't have it correct, then circle and fix that part of the problem."

Repeat the above statement for each part of the problem, until all parts of the problem have been processed.

Reflection

9. Say to the students: "Write a reflective statement on your paper that is a complete sentence that matches the stars and circles for problem number one."

"Stand up when you have written your reflection."

When all students have stood up, say "Share your reflection with a neighbor."

10. Circulate through the room listening for an example of a good reflection written by a student.

Have one or two students who have written good reflections share their reflections with the class.

Have all students sit down.

Key Idea Statement

11. Say to the students: "Write the key idea statement for the category on your paper as I write it on the board. Stand up when you're finished."

Have the students say the key idea statement to their partner. Then repeat the key idea statement together as a class. Have the students sit down. This ends the processing for problem number one.

12. Follow the same routine for all the problems in the math review.

Overall Reflection for the Day (Optional)

13. Say to the students: "Write one or two sentences at the bottom of your paper indicating how you did on math review today. Did you make an improvement on certain problems? Did you discover something about your math ability that you didn't know before?"

Script for the Student-Directed Method

1. Students indicate their designated partner.

2. Students write their name, the date, and the title "Math Review" on their papers.

3. Students work with their partners for eight minutes to complete the math review problems. During the eight minutes of work time, the teacher circulates throughout the classroom looking for student pairs to invite to process the math review problems with the class.

4. At the end of eight minutes, students stop working on the math review problems, put away their pencils, and hold up their marking pens. It's OK if students are not finished with the problems. At this point, the teachers need to place themselves at the back of the room to facilitate the student-directed process. This process doesn't work well if the teacher remains at the front of the classroom and interrupts the student explanations.

Following Directions

5. The first student pair comes to the front of the room and begins with the feedback for following directions: The student pair asks the rest of the class to put a star beside their names, the date, and the title "Math Review," and to check their partner's paper to see if those elements are in place. The student pair tells the class, "Say to your partner 'you are good at following directions' or 'you need to follow directions,'" then tell the class they should check to see if they numbered their problems, copied the problems on their paper, and showed all of their work. The pair says to the class, "If you did, write 'I'm awesome at following directions' on your paper. If you didn't do all those things, write 'I need to follow directions' on your paper."

Error Analysis

6. The student pair now starts the error analysis portion. This becomes an "agree/disagree" process when students are providing the error analysis. Students will write on the board what they think is the first portion of the solution. Then they say to the class, "How many agree?" and then they say to the class, "How many disagree?" The teacher needs to monitor if all students are making a decision either to agree or to disagree. Student pairs can call on one or two students to ask why they agree or disagree.

The process of starring each part of the solution that is correct and circling and fixing each part of the problem that is incorrect remains the same.

Reflection

7. The student pair now directs the class to write a one-sentence reflection based on the feedback that they just received from starring and circling and fixing key parts of the problem. The student pair says to the class, "Stand up when you have written your reflection and then we will select two people to share their reflections." As soon as all students are finished writing their reflections and are standing, each student presenter selects one of their classmates to share their reflections orally.

Key Idea Statement

8. The student pair asks the class to write the key idea statement on their paper and then stand up. Then they lead the class in saying the key idea statement to their respective partners and then together as a whole class.

9. At this point, the teacher leads the class in congratulating the student pair for a fine job and the next student pair moves to the front of the room to process problem number two. The second and third student pairs (or more if you're doing more than three problems on your classroom math review) follow the same process, but they omit the "following directions" section.

Math review process scripts are available in Appendix B, and the math review feedback form is available in Appendix C.

Variations for Early Grades

Some components of the math review process need to be modified for prekindergarten, kindergarten, and first and second grades, but the essential components are still present in the process. The primary grades build the foundation for the process, impressing upon students early on that "in math class we work on problems together, we have math conversations, we all have good ideas about numbers, and it is OK to make mistakes when you're learning math."

Kindergarten and Prekindergarten

- Students sit on the rug close to the teacher.
- Students have a designated partner.
- Categories and problems are based on number sense.
- Students have necessary manipulatives for categories.

Categories are completed one at a time using the following sequence:

- The teacher reads problem number one to the students and then the students and the teacher read the problem together.
- Students try the problem independently for a couple of minutes using the available manipulatives.
- Students turn to face their partners and discuss what they tried and what they think the answer is.

- Students turn back to face the teacher and the class solves the problem together. This provides timely and specific feedback for the students.

- Students turn to their partner and participate in reflection by sharing how they did on the problem.

- The class says the key idea statement for the problem together two times.

The same sequence is followed for problems two and three.

Assessment for prekindergarten and kindergarten is based on teacher observation. It does not include the formal data collection described for the other grade levels. A way to structure the informal formative assessment is to select an interval of days of when to observe and decide if the students are proficient with a category. For example, many kindergarten teachers that I work with find that every fifth or sixth day is a good interval to use. So, after a category has been practiced for six days by the students, the teacher will check to see how the students are doing and make anecdotal notes about that category to decide if the category can be changed or not. An easy way to check is to provide a longer period of time in the sequence when the students are trying the problem independently and observe how many students are successful.

First Grade

At the beginning of the year, first-grade math review may need to look like what was described for kindergarten math review to build student capacity for the process.

- Students sit on the rug or in desks close to the teacher.

- Students have a designated partner.

- Categories and problems are based on number sense.

- Students have necessary manipulatives for categories.

- Students have a paper template to record work.

Categories are completed one at a time using the following sequence:

- The teacher reads problem number one to the students and then the students and the teacher read the problem together.

- Students try the problem independently for a couple of minutes using the available manipulatives and paper and pencil.

- Students turn to face their partners and discuss what they tried and what they think the answer is and record on their paper what they tried.

- Students turn back to face the teacher and the class solves the problem together, providing timely and specific feedback for the students. The students star work that is correct on their paper and circle and fix work that is incorrect or incomplete.

- Students turn to their partners and participate in reflection by sharing how they did on the problem.

- The class says the key idea statement for the problem together two times.

The same sequence is followed for problems two and three.

The assessment component for first grade is the same as described in the math review quiz section for other grade levels in the coming pages.

Second Grade

Math review for second grade may need to look like the math review process described for first grade at the beginning of the year to build student capacity. When the students are ready, math review for second grade is the same as math review described for all grade levels in the previous section with the exception that the key idea statement is orally repeated, not written. Second-grade students will solve and process all three problems together, not do them one at a time like first-grade students, and they will write their own reflections using sentence starters.

The second-grade assessment is the same as the math review quiz for all other grade levels.

Variations for Advanced Courses

The math review process is very effective for mathematics courses above algebra I, but a few variations are necessary. Typically, two problems instead of three problems fit the 15-minute time frame, because of the complexity of the problems in higher-level math courses. All the key components still remain as part of the structure. What changes is the category selection and the emphasis in the error analysis phase. The categories should represent what the teacher feels are key concepts for success in the given course and what concepts tend to cause confusion for a majority of students. The error analysis and student work should begin to emphasize verification of solution as the year progresses so that developing viable arguments and responding to those arguments becomes the basis of student discourse during the math review work time.

The Math Review Quiz

The math review process must be data driven or it isn't effective. The math review quiz will provide the data necessary for the decisions that need to be made about student proficiency and the changing of the math review categories.

The math review quiz should be administered once a week or once every two weeks depending on the grade level. In the K–2 grade span it may be advantageous to quiz students once a week. (Note that in kindergarten, students will not be given a formal paper and pencil quiz. The kindergarten quiz process was described in the "variations for early grades" section.) Quizzes every other week are effective for all other grade levels.

Basically, math review is a 10-day cycle: three days of the teacher-directed method, six days of the student-directed method, then on the tenth day the math review quiz is administered.

The quiz contains problems from the categories that have been practiced during math review the previous nine days. Most teachers implement math review using three categories, which means that to develop a fair assessment, you would need to have four problems for each category. The problems need to be structured the same way they were in math review during the prior nine days, just with different numbers. The math review quiz is not meant to assess the key idea statements, and also doesn't involve the regular reflection piece. It's best to write out the quiz and make copies for the students so that the assessment format doesn't involve students copying problems from another source and the issues that can result from that situation for students. On the day that the quiz is administered, the regular math review process is not completed.

The math review quiz is passed out to students and they complete the problems independently within a given amount of time. The quiz will take a little longer than regular math review, but the teacher will have to determine a stopping point for everyone. Keep in mind that the students have practiced the problems in the categories for nine days with very specific feedback. They either know the problems or they don't. An extended amount of time doesn't tend to change that situation for the student.

When students are finished with the math review quiz, I recommend that the quiz be graded with the students using the same system of error analysis they have been experiencing on a daily basis during math review. Over the years I have found that grading the quiz with the students increases student engagement and student responsibility with the entire process. Students use their regular marking pen to go through the error analysis pertaining to each problem. It is recommended that no partial credit be given on problems, so that the data collected from the quiz will be informative about which students know a given problem and which students don't know the problem. If a student misses anything on a given problem, then that problem is considered incorrect. At the end of the grading process, students can record their score at the top of their paper, and on the back of the paper each student either congratulates themselves for a great performance or writes a plan for improvement to deal with the mistakes that were made on the quiz. Of course, the teacher will still need to look at the quizzes to check for correctness.

Use of the Math Review Quiz Data

Math review quiz data can be used for two important decisions within the math review process. The first is to determine individual student proficiency on the quiz. This allows the teacher to decide which students are doing well in the process and which students need some extra assistance. Most schools and districts that implement math review use 80 percent as the necessary level of performance for proficiency. If any students are below 80 percent, then they become eligible for extra support processes that are explained below.

The second important use of the data is to determine which math review categories will change and which categories need to stay on math review a while longer.

The standard to change a category is that 90 percent of the students need to obtain 100 percent proficiency on that category on the math review quiz. That means if there are four problems for a category on the math review quiz, then 90 percent of the students in the class have to get all four problems correct for that category to be changed and removed from math review. Of course, this standard is not set in stone. As you start assessing, you may feel the need to change the standard slightly. Just be careful that the change that is made doesn't create a situation where students are left behind in the process and their misconceptions are not addressed.

Math Review Interventions

The following are possible interventions for students achieving less than 80 percent proficiency:

Flex Groups

The first intervention suggestion involves flex grouping. After grading the math review quiz, the teacher lists those students who scored below 80 percent. The next day in class, the listed students will be with the teacher during the eight minutes that are used by students to work the problems in a flex group. For a few days the teacher will meet with this flex group and support them with the current math review. After a few days, the students go back to their regular partners. Obviously, there will have to be a few adjustments made with student partners during the days that there is a flex group operating. The wonderful side benefit of this process is that the students who are in the flex group many times become a support to each other, which starts building the students' belief in their own efficacy immediately.

New Partner

In the case of a student continuing to have low performance over a couple of quizzes, it's usually advantageous to change their partner to someone who will be more helpful and supportive to them. A suggestion for this process is to develop a list of students in your class who you consider to have the characteristics of mentors. You can offer the struggling student a choice from the mentor list for a new partner.

Retaking the Quiz After Help Is Provided

Over the years, and across many grade levels, I have found that this intervention has by far the greatest positive impact on student attitude and belief in their efficacy. The process I used in my classroom at both elementary and secondary levels was that if a student scored less than 80 percent on a math review quiz they became eligible to retake the quiz after receiving help within a given window of time.

Usually, students were given a two-week window to take care of getting help and retesting. I facilitated retesting by creating an "A" and "B" version of the math review quiz when it was developed. Basically students would receive help during the help sessions I offered using the quiz on which they scored less than proficient. Then after two or three help sessions, the students would retake the quiz. If their performance was better, they received the improved scores. Students were only given one opportunity to retest.

Of course, this type of intervention is dependent upon finding ways in your school schedule and school culture to offer help sessions. Educators also may have to wrestle with their own issues pertaining to retesting, because some feel that the practice is somehow not fair, not useful, or too much work. I was always amazed at how powerful this practice was with students who had struggled. When I was in a secondary setting, many students didn't believe that it was really possible to have a second chance with a math assessment, but once they tried it, their attitude and feeling of hope would change. The students started to believe that they could succeed in a subject that they had been avoiding and telling themselves they couldn't do for years.

These suggestions for intervention are just that—suggestions. There are many ways to provide extra help to students, but of primary importance is that it is decided at the school or district level what happens to students that are not proficient on the quiz. What is our plan? How will that plan be carried out on a regular basis? If there is no plan, students are left with their misconceptions and continue on their path of struggle and eventually failure.

Ninth Period—A Model for Intervention

The math review model is very effective in intervention situations. Students who are struggling react in a positive fashion to the features of this process that give them daily practice coupled with specific feedback focused on skills that they may have been having trouble with for years.

An effective example of this idea was demonstrated by Dr. Frank Klajda, former principal at Fees College Preparatory Middle School in Tempe Elementary School District, and his staff when they created what they called ninth period. During ninth period, students would be assigned either to intervention or to enrichment. The ninth period had been created by adjusting other periods by a few minutes each day. The intervention process for math was impressive. The math department developed what were called survival categories for grades 6, 7, and 8 using algebra I as the end product for all students. The intervention class was taught by the math teachers and the math review process was used as the instructional tool. The students did one formal math review a day, then a second math review as a practice. The modification that made a difference in student progress was assessing the students in intervention more often to provide more regular feedback.

Mental Math—A Daily Process to Develop Number Sense

Mental Math is an engaging daily process that takes only a few minutes. It provides students with a risk-free opportunity to develop better number sense, build capacity for upcoming units of instruction, and gain general knowledge they may be lacking. It works at any grade level and typically hooks kids immediately if it is done with enthusiasm and student success in mind. In my classroom, I usually did two or three mental math problems a day.

My version of mental math involves saying a string of operations with numbers that are based on a number pattern theme to students verbally and having the students do the necessary manipulations in their minds to find a solution. The only part of mental math that is written is the solution. Here is an example of a mental math problem: The teacher would say to students: multiply three times two; now multiply that answer times 10; then multiply *that* answer times 10; write down your answer.

The Sequence for Mental Math

The teacher says the mental math problem once and tells students to write down their answers, if they have answers. If students do not have answers, the problem will be repeated so they will have another opportunity to find the answer. Then the teacher says the mental math problem a second time.

To process the answer, it's not a good idea to call on individuals. It's much better to get group responses and then ask a student who was correct to share the thinking behind the solution. For example, the teacher can count to three and have all students say out their answers and then verify the correct response. Another alternative is to have students share their answers with a person they are seated next to and have them explain their reasoning. The last suggestion is also diagnostic in nature. The teacher says, "How many got a certain number," to find out if students made a common mistake or if their answers are unreasonable. It's quick and easy formative information about students' number sense at a certain grade level. For the mental math example above, the teacher could say to the students: "How many got 26?"; "How many got 60?"; "How many got 6000?"; and "How many got 600?" Of course, it would be divulged what is correct. Then a student is selected to share the correct reasoning. The best way to facilitate student metacognitive sharing is to repeat the mental math problem to the selected student one step at a time and have the student share the thoughts and mathematical principles that led to the correct answer.

Choosing a Theme

The idea of having a theme for mental math is to find a pattern in the number system or a number sense theme that will benefit students at the grade level you are teaching. You will need to stay with a theme for at least two weeks, or at least until students have internalized the theme enough for it to become useful in their computation work. One method to find a theme is to consider the next instructional unit on the horizon and decide what number pattern or property of the number system would be beneficial to the students as they work through that unit. Then you do mental math based on that theme a few weeks before getting to the next unit and build student capacity that otherwise wouldn't be there. I call it "front-end loading." Students really respond to the process because of the confidence that they have already developed before they see the information in the next instructional unit. My favorite example is when I knew I was headed toward teaching the Pythagorean theorem, I would spend a few weeks prior working with square numbers and square roots in mental math. The students' prior experience in the mental math exercises allowed them to concentrate on the relationships in right triangles during that unit, as opposed to getting stuck struggling with square numbers and square roots.

Examples of themes:

- Basic math facts in all four operations
- Inverse relationship of operations
- Multiples of 10
- Making 10
- One more than, one less than
- Doubles
- Near doubles
- Square numbers, square roots
- Vocabulary and geometry
- Measurement units
- Fractional parts of a whole

Mental Math in Kindergarten and First Grade

Mental math in kindergarten and first grade is lots of fun. It's the same idea but the number themes are presented within a story context. The themes should be based in number sense, but to present the problem, use names of the students and contexts that they are interested in and tell the mental math problem as a story. It's a great experience for kids that age.

Implementation

Mental math should be a daily activity. You will find that if you try it, students will like it, and they will remind you to do it if you forget. What makes mental math powerful is the daily practice it gives students and the way that it keeps them engaged in number sense development in particular and math learning in general.

CHAPTER 2

Problem Solving

"A teacher of mathematics has a great opportunity. If he fills his allotted time with drilling his students in routine operations, he kills their interest, hampers their intellectual development, and misuses his opportunity. But if he challenges the curiosity of his students by setting them problems proportionate to their knowledge, and helps them to solve their problems with stimulating questions, he may give them a taste for, and some means of, independent thinking."

—**George Polya, 1945** (Ben-Hur, 2006, p. 76)

What Is Problem Solving?

Problem solving, for the purposes of the methods being described here, refers to students working on mathematical problems that can be solved multiple ways and typically involve more than one mathematical concept. This type of problem solving is a "messy" process and involves classroom instructional time. An important element of effective problem solving is that it involves students struggling with mathematical ideas as opposed to students waiting for the teacher to explain the correct pathway to the solution. The methods that will be described in the coming pages are not "canned approaches" that give students the idea that a solution is found by following a particular series of steps; rather, these methods promote the idea that all students are capable of applying the mathematical concepts they are learning to contextual situations, and that capacity can be further developed. A good task for this type of problem solving will be matched to the unit of instruction, will allow for various paths to the solution, and will be at the middle range of ability for the class to allow for success.

The goals for problem solving are for students to be able to:

• Develop problem analysis skills

- Develop and be able to select strategies

- Justify solutions

- Extend and generalize patterns developed within problems

- Gain confidence and belief in their efficacy (the capacity to produce a desired effect)

- Be willing to try and persevere (become tenacious)

- Enjoy doing math (engagement, attitude)

The Case for Teaching Problem Solving

In *Adding It Up* (2001) by the National Research Council, one of the cornerstone documents of the Common Core State Standards for Mathematics, the authors discuss mathematical proficiency—what they believe is necessary for anyone to learn mathematics successfully. They label one of the necessary strands as "strategic competence" and define it as "the ability to formulate mathematical problems, represent them, and solve them" (p. 124).

Another aspect of the Common Core that must be considered in classroom instruction is the inclusion of the Standards for Mathematical Practice that define the types of practices that need to be part of daily instruction for students to be mathematically proficient. There are direct connections between the Standards for Mathematical Practice and the problem-solving methods that will be described in this chapter. The poster method, the poster method with a write-up, and the alternative method that will be described in the coming pages, when integrated into a consistent, structured classroom problem-solving program, will introduce these six mathematical practices from the Common Core into the classroom environment:

- Solve problems

- Reason abstractly and quantitatively

- Construct viable arguments

- Model with mathematics

- Use tools strategically

- Attend to precision

Myths About Problem Solving

Over the years, problem solving has been taught in various ways in U.S. classrooms, and sometimes not taught at all. The approaches to problem solving promoted in math textbook series have created various beliefs about how students learn problem solving, depending on the confidence level of the teacher in the area of problem solving. In my experience, I've found that there is wide variation in educators' belief in students' capacity to even do problem solving in mathematics. These kinds of beliefs can stop instruction in problem solving—a wonderful, beneficial activity—from actually taking place at all.

Myth 1: There Is One Way to Solve a Given Problem

This myth refers to textbook approaches that give the impression that a problem is solved a given way, and that's how it is presented by the teacher. Students get the impression that if they can find the magic way that a problem is solved, then they can just use that method and they are set. Or, students spend all their time trying to remember the exact method that should work with a given problem and they don't make any progress with actually solving the problem they're trying to work on. Problem-solving tasks can be solved a variety of ways. Students should be aware of various strategies that can be useful so that they have a tool kit to draw from when solving. A given problem doesn't have a particular given strategy that must be used.

Myth 2: The Teacher's Way or the Highway

Another issue connected to this is that in some classrooms students get the impression that there is just one way to solve a problem—the teacher's way. Especially for younger children, this can be very detrimental to not only their confidence with problem solving but also their idea of what math problem solving is about. The main issue is that the students' thinking is not honored, or many times does not become part of the learning environment during problem solving. They walk away from the experience thinking that what they were trying in their minds is wrong and that they can't do math.

Myth 3: Problem Solving Should Be Nice and Neat and Quick

This myth needs to be addressed at the beginning of the implementation of any problem-solving program or problem-solving method. Problem solving takes time, and is not a nice neat package that can be presented to students as a set of steps to follow that will automatically create success. Problem solving involves struggle, thinking, reasoning, collaboration, justification, and metacognitive practice—all processes that are extremely valuable to student learning but are not easily developed in a climate of covering a text-book or doing a lesson a day.

The procedural approach to teaching mathematics in the United Sates that has been followed for decades has created a situation where many teachers feel that they need to show students a set of steps that lead to an answer, have them practice, and then move on to the next concept so they can cover their course material or curriculum. (It's the at-titude projected from that old saying about dividing fractions—"Don't wonder why, just invert and multiply.") When the idea of taking a class period to do "messy problem solving" is presented, the immediate objections will be that taking a whole class period to do problem solving will stop them from covering the material, and that they can't imagine the benefit. Considering the expectations about problem solving presented in the Common Core State Standards, or even just in the Standards for Mathematical Prac-tice, this issue has to be discussed, and those underlying beliefs must be addressed or the implementation of problem-solving instruction will be quite difficult.

Problem solving is actually more beneficial and effective for students learning math-ematics than the "cover all the material" instructional model. Teaching problem solving is extremely valuable to the teacher from the standpoint of diagnosing misconception, gaining formative information about the effectiveness of instruction, and getting to know students mathematically. The tradition of covering all the material in a textbook just to cover material has no basis in educational or learning theory to support the prac-tice. You might think of it like this: those who are just covering the text are teaching the course, but they definitely are not teaching the students.

For students, problem solving is beneficial to developing understanding, allows for application of the mathematics that is being learned, promotes students' belief in their efficacy and a positive attitude about mathematics, and provides a vehicle for students to discover the utility of learning mathematics.

Myth 4: If You Can't Remember the Formula, There Is No Hope of Solving the Problem

The procedural approach to teaching mathematics that has been prevalent in the United States for decades has created an approach to problem solving for many people that tends to stop them before they even get started with trying to understand the problem or begin the reasoning process. Many people believe that if they can't remember a specific formula that fits the problem they are working on, then there is no hope of find-ing a solution, so they don't even start to try. Learning mathematics as a set of rules to get an answer without understanding why the procedure works makes people think that there has to be a step-by-step process that doesn't involve any reasoning that they can follow to reach a solution. They just have to remember what that process is. Adults and students with that belief or approach find problem solving frustrating and almost impossible.

Research

The basic research on problem solving in mathematics can be traced to the work of George Polya in the 1940s. His description of the problem-solving process and the components involved can be very helpful when integrating problem solving into classroom instruction.

According to Polya, the problem-solving process involves (Ben-Hur, 2006, p. 83):

- Understanding the problem and identifying the target goal

- Translating verbal and other information into mathematical language without changing the meaning

- Planning a solution

- Solving the problem

- Reviewing and evaluating the solution in the context of the problem

He also thought that problem solving is not a linear process that can be memorized, practiced, and habituated. At any point in the process, the solver may reexamine the given data, change the data back and forth across different representations, shift strategies, and correct a solution more than once.

In terms of the demands on the student, problem solving requires analysis and reasoning that is goal-oriented and self-motivated. Also, students must learn to gather information in careful, systematic, and precise ways. Most importantly, students must understand what they read to be able to define the problem they are pursuing.

Another useful thought from research targets the area of justification, which is emphasized in the Common Core but typically not taught: "Reviewing the solution—looking back at a solution to check the result, check the argument, derive the results differently, use the result or the method for some other problem, reinterpret the result, or state a new problem—is the focus of what Dewey (1933) and Polya (1945) described as the most critical step in problem solving" (Ben-Hur, 2006).

Typical Problem-Solving Strategies

Students should be aware of different ways to solve problems and should have experience with different strategies, but they should never be given the impression that a given problem-solving task should be solved with a particular problem-solving strategy. That type of approach is counterproductive for the student, and encourages the student to spend much of the problem-solving time searching for the strategy that matches the problem instead of attempting to solve the problem. Below is a list of problem-solving strategies to provide to students.

- Draw a picture
- Look for a pattern
- Make a table or chart
- Try a simpler form of the problem
- Guess and check
- Make an organized list

Classroom Environment and Instructional Practices

The traditional math classroom dominated by a teacher telling students how to do procedures to find solutions is not conducive to the problem-solving process for students. Listed below are thoughts and suggestions that should be discussed and considered during implementation of problem-solving instruction:

- Classroom communication is of critical importance to the learning process in mathematics.
- Teachers need to create an atmosphere of legitimacy for being wrong and making errors.
- Students should be encouraged to participate in verbal discourse and writing pertaining to mathematical ideas.
- Teachers need to require justification of student responses to raise the level of reasoning and to challenge and value student thinking.
- Teachers should listen actively to become student centered.
- Instruction should be focused on Big Ideas and connections instead of individual terms in standards.

- Teachers should move away from the "telling" method of teaching math to create intellectual curiosity with mathematics.

- It is a good idea to allow students to find generalizations by studying patterns (math facts, formulas).

- Teachers should include vocabulary instruction in their lessons.

Teachers' expectations of their students for a given subject are extremely powerful in terms of the students' attitudes about and performance in that subject. Here are some suggestions to help students develop belief in their own efficacy toward problem solving in mathematics:

- Have high expectations of all students.

- Respect students' thoughts by listening to their ideas and honoring those ideas.

- Praise student effort and risk taking within the problem-solving process.

- Build success with problem solving by focusing on student thinking and reasoning.

- Listen to all students by creating an environment that facilitates discourse, metacognitive practice, and student voice, and that de-emphasizes teacher voice.

- Provide special successes for special children.

Here are some general ideas about problem solving that are good to keep in mind during the implementation of a problem-solving program:

- If students are to learn how to solve problems, teachers must engage them with real problems on a regular basis.

- Problem solving is not just a means for finding a correct answer; it is a vehicle for developing logical thinking and an opportunity for transfer of newly acquired concepts and ideas.

- It is OK to not know right away.

- Student reasoning and thinking should be honored.

- Students struggling to solve problems is good and productive.

- Problem solving is a collaborative, active, and messy process.

- The environment established by the math review process is well suited for problem solving.

To Save or Not to Save

"Instruction should not seek to automate students' problem solving through the teaching of algorithms and tricks that work for given types of problems. Rather it should attempt to provoke students' cognitive dissonance and at the same time enhance cognitive competence" (Ben-Hur, 2006).

During a problem-solving session with students, the teacher has a role that for many educators feels uncomfortable. The typical role that teachers take during problem solving is that of "saving" students during problem solving any time that a student begins to struggle or feel any frustration. For teachers to effectively turn their students into strong, confident problem solvers, teachers will need to take the following actions in the classroom:

- Guide, coach, and ask insightful questions as well as help students develop independence.
- Elicit discussions around students' ideas and beliefs about the topic.
- Make provisions for learners to be able to clarify their ideas or beliefs through small-group work.
- Promote metacognitive discourse among students.
- Listen carefully to student conversation to diagnose student understanding and misconception.
- Keep students on task.
- Make sure that they do not interfere with students' problem-solving process.

Guiding Questions

The following questions enhance students' metacognition, which can help them succeed, but do not "save" students:

- What are you doing?
- Why are you doing it?
- How does it help you?
- What did you do that helped you understand the problem?
- Did you find information that you didn't need?
- How did you decide what to do?
- How did you decide your answer was correct?

Teacher Preparation

Taking the following actions before starting a problem-solving activity with students can help teachers prepare for the lesson:

- Do the problem yourself.
- Try to solve the problem several ways using several strategies.
- Think of possible student misconceptions.
- Develop a mathematical justification for the solution to the problem.
- Become a problem solver as a powerful model for students and to build personal belief in efficacy.

Issues that Impede Implementation of Problem Solving

Students Giving Up or Not Being Willing to Try

Each year that passes without students gaining problem-solving experience and success with problem solving creates an ever-increasing negative situation. Students in this situation will develop defensive behaviors that they think will protect them from the perceived embarrassment they fear will be associated with not being able to solve a problem. When implementing a problem-solving program in upper elementary and secondary grades, consideration has to be given to the reason that many students won't try at all or give up if they don't find an answer quickly. What will change this situation quickly is a supportive environment, immediate success, and a focus on student ideas and reasoning as opposed to only the answer.

Teacher Expectations

Teacher expectations are a very important factor when implementing problem-solving methods in the classroom. Students are very aware of what adults think they can do, and their performance can be either negatively or positively impacted by these adult expectations. Part of the implementation process will need to be a reflective discussion with teachers about their belief about students' problem-solving abilities and how that belief influences their actions in the classroom. The methods described in *Balancing Mathematics Instruction* are based on the belief that all students have the natural ability to solve problems in mathematics and that all students can learn to be proficient at problem solving. Problem-solving instructional methods have the teachers acting as facilitators of the process, not inserting themselves into the student collaborative groups and telling frustrated students how to proceed. In this role, teachers are demonstrating their belief in the students' abilities, which creates an atmosphere that supports the development of students' belief in their own efficacy.

Lack of Student Engagement

If the problem-solving experience for students is designed around the factors of how people learn and how students are engaged, then students, even reluctant students, will participate in the process and gain experience and a positive attitude. But if the problem-solving environment or process loses any of the elements of discourse, collaboration, and support, the students will be unengaged and reluctant to pursue problem solving.

Key Word Approach

If students have experienced several years of being told that one of the first steps in problem solving is to look for key words in the problem and that those key words indicate a mathematical operation, they develop an unworkable view of the problem-solving process. The key word approach leads students to the idea that they just have to find the "magic" word in the problem that will tell them what to do, then they can perform that mathematical operation on the numbers in the problem and they have their answer. The key word approach actually hinders the natural problem-solving ability that students have because it moves them away from initially just trying to understand the context of the problem. Students also get the impression that problem solving isn't a messy process during which they might have to try several strategies and might have to start over several times to find a solution. It would be much better to train students to read the problem several times, looking for information that will help them understand the problem and what they are being asked to do.

Problems Matched to a Strategy Method

Many math textbook approaches to problem solving can give students the impression that a given problem should be solved using a particular strategy. A very common structure that students will have experienced is that there is one problem-solving task presented within a chapter in a textbook and that task is directly linked to a given strategy to be used to reach a solution. If that is the only problem solving that students participate in, they can easily develop the idea that problems have a matching strategy that should be used to solve the problem. This impression becomes very constraining, to the point of stopping students from proceeding when they try problem solving independently. Instead of beginning their problem-solving process by trying to understand the problem and then thinking of various strategies they might try, students with the described impression will spend their time trying to discern which strategy matches this problem, because they believe there has to be a match in order for them to find the answer. They may never get beyond that point in the process. Students should be taught about different strategies, but it is essential that they aren't led to believe that a given problem has to be solved using a certain strategy.

Connections to the Common Core Mathematical Practice Standards

Problem solving is directly linked to several of the Standards for Mathematical Practice that are an integral component of the Common Core State Standards for Mathematics. If you are teaching in a state that has not adopted the Common Core, the problem-solving methods presented here are still an effective means to develop the components of mathematical proficiency, as defined by the authors of *Adding It Up* (2001) by the National Research Council.

The problem-solving methods described in the following pages, when implemented with fidelity, provide a vehicle to infuse several of the Common Core's Standards for Mathematical Practice into a math classroom. The practice standards are listed below in bold, followed by wording from the description of each practice standard that relates directly to problem solving (National Governors Association Center for Best Practices and Council of Chief State School Officers, 2010).

Make Sense of Problems and Persevere in Solving Them

- "Mathematically proficient students start by explaining to themselves the meaning of a problem and looking for entry points to its solution."

- "They make conjectures about the form and meaning of the solution and plan a solution pathway rather than simply jumping into a solution attempt."

- "They monitor and evaluate their progress and change course if necessary."

- "Mathematically proficient students check their answers to problems using a different method, and they continually ask themselves, 'Does this make sense?'"

Reason Abstractly and Quantitatively

- "Mathematically proficient students make sense of quantities and their relationships in problem situations."

- "They [have] … the ability to *decontextualize*—to abstract a given situation and represent it symbolically and manipulate the representing symbols as if they have a life of their own."

Construct Viable Arguments and Critique the Reasoning of Others

- "Mathematically proficient students understand and use stated assumptions, definitions, and previously established results in constructing arguments."

- "They justify their conclusions, communicate them to others, and respond to the arguments of others."

- "Students at all grades can listen or read the arguments of others, decide whether they make sense, and ask useful questions to clarify or improve the arguments."

Model with Mathematics

- "Mathematically proficient students can apply the mathematics they know to solve problems arising in everyday life, society, and the workplace."

- "They are able to identify important quantities in a practical situation and map their relationships using such tools as diagrams, two-way tables, graphs, flowcharts and formulas. They can analyze those relationships to draw conclusions."

Use Appropriate Tools Strategically

- "Mathematically proficient students consider the available tools when solving a mathematical problem."

- "Proficient students are sufficiently familiar with tools appropriate for their grade or course to make sound decisions about when each of these tools might be helpful, recognizing both the insight to be gained and their limitations."

Attend to Precision

- "Mathematically proficient students try to communicate precisely to others. They try to use clear definitions in discussion with others and in their own reasoning."

- "They calculate accurately and efficiently, [and] express numerical answers with a degree of precision appropriate for the problem context."

Connections to Elements of Mathematical Proficiency

Problem solving connects directly to the elements of mathematical proficiency listed in *Adding It Up* (2001) by the National Research Council. The elements are shown in bold, followed by wording describing each element.

Conceptual Understanding

- "They understand why a mathematical idea is important and the kinds of contexts in which it is useful."

- "A significant indicator of conceptual understanding is being able to represent mathematical situations in different ways and knowing how different representations can be useful for different purposes."

Strategic Competence

- "Strategic competence refers to the ability to formulate mathematical problems, represent them, and solve them."

- "They are likely to need experience and practice in problem formulating as well as in problem solving."

- "A fundamental characteristic needed throughout the problem-solving process is flexibility. Flexibility develops through the broadening of knowledge required for solving nonroutine problems rather than just routine problems."

Adaptive Reasoning

- "Adaptive reasoning refers to the capacity to think logically about the relationships among concepts and situations."

- "One manifestation of adaptive reasoning is the ability to justify one's work."

- "Classroom norms can be established in which students are expected to justify their mathematical claims and make them clear to others."

- "Students need to be able to justify and explain ideas in order to make their reasoning clear, hone their reasoning skills, and improve their conceptual understanding."

Productive Disposition

- "Mathematically proficient people believe that mathematics should make sense, that they can figure it out, that they can solve mathematical problems by working hard on them, and that becoming mathematically proficient is worth the effort."

Developing a Problem-Solving Program

Here is a suggested sequence to follow to develop an effective problem-solving program that can be implemented by one teacher, a grade level, a school, or a district:

1. Develop a student product format with consistent expectations. Consider where and how students will show their work, how students will record what they did with other students, and how students will explain their final solution and their justification of that solution.

2. Develop a plan to provide students with experience using various problem-solving strategies.

3. Develop a plan to develop student capacity for problem solving that includes support and success and leads to students' belief in their own problem-solving efficacy.

4. Decide which methods to use to involve students in problem solving and the sequence of those methods.

5. Decide how students will share their solutions and how the correct solution will be determined in class.

6. Decide how often to do problem solving. How will it fit into the schedule on a regular basis?

7. Develop a general rubric, or scoring guide, that is consistent across the grade level, school, or district.

8. Find sources of problems and a method to collect effective problem solving tasks.

Problem-Solving Methods that Work

Listed below, in sequence, are three problem-solving methods that build and enhance students' capacity to solve problems in mathematics.

When teaching students to use a new problem-solving method, it is a good idea to have them practice one component of the method for a few minutes each day for a week, and then move on to the next component. This works for all grade levels. It's best to teach the poster method first, because it involves training students in such skills as collaboration and on-task conversation, which will be useful not only for the other problem-solving methods, but also for other mathematical instruction strategies.

Examples of these methods are available on the DVD included with this book.

The Poster Method

The poster method is a collaborative problem-solving method that includes developing a group solution, creating a written explanation of the solution, developing a viable argument defending the group's solution, and engaging in mathematical discourse through discussion of others' solutions.

To be successful with the poster method, students will need training in:

Collaboration: Students need to know what it means to do a task in a collaborative situation and then must practice this skill several times before doing problem solving.

On-task conversation: Define what on-task conversation means in your classroom environment, practice the skill, and then strictly enforce that expectation during problem solving.

Written explanation in mathematics: Students need practice with how to describe their mathematical reasoning in written form. It can be very helpful to do some descriptions together as a class so that students have a model of a written explanation in mathematics. The goal should be a detailed description of student thinking with correct use of mathematical terminology, but that will take practice. Be patient.

Data sheet process: All three problem-solving methods presented here involve the use of a "data sheet." A data sheet is a paper for students to use to record the thoughts, calculations, and graphic representations that they generate in the process of solving a problem. In other words, it's where students can "dump out their brains" while problem solving. Training students to use a data sheet is critical because students have to feel comfortable recording any ideas they have, whether those ideas are correct or not. The tremendous value of the data sheet is that it shows students the pathway they took to get to the solution for a problem. Problem solving isn't a straight-line process. It involves starting, stopping, rethinking, and modifying. The data sheet allows students to have a record of their journey and it also facilitates metacognitive practice.

A Sequence for the Poster Method

1. Students should be in groups of three or four.

2. Each student needs an individual piece of paper, to be labeled "data sheet," and a pencil.

3. Explain to students what a data sheet is and how to use one. (A data sheet is a place to record your thoughts about solving a problem. It doesn't matter if the ideas are correct or not. Write down anything that you try.)

4. Read the problem to the students. Read the problem with the students twice.

5. Have the students try the problem individually for eight to 10 minutes.

6. Have students stop working and write two complete sentences on their individual data sheets about what they did to try to solve the problem. Students stand up when they are finished writing.

7. When all students are standing, have two or three students read their sentences to the class. Do not comment on the sentences. Simply say, "Thank you for sharing." These sentences provide information for all students to consider as they move into the collaborative part of this method.

8. Have students work in their groups to solve the problem and try to reach agreement on a solution. It's fine if they can't agree. They can agree to disagree.

9. Provide students with poster paper and marking pens.

10. Have students create a group data sheet that indicates the group's solution (or solutions, if they can't agree) and ideas from each member of the group.

11. Before the group data sheets are complete, do the "visit." The visit involves one student remaining at their group's location to explain the ideas on the group data sheet. The remaining group members visit other groups to discuss their ideas about solving the problem (two to three minutes).

12. Everyone returns to their group. Each group has a brief discussion about the visit and makes a decision about their solution. Do they want to change their solution or stay with their solution?

13. Have students finalize the group data sheets.

14. Have students complete the written explanation on the back of the group data sheet. Students answer the following questions in detail: How did your group solve the problem? How does your group know the answer is correct mathematically?

15. Provide rehearsal time for the "circle discussion" if necessary.

16. Circle discussion: All groups state their solution. Have a group that is confident about their solution defend their solution. Start the math discussion by asking which groups agree and which groups disagree. Call on groups to say why they agree or disagree. The teacher's role is to ask questions to keep the discussion going, but not to comment on anything being stated by students.

17. Use a group data sheet to explain the correct solution to the class.

Components of the Poster Method and Their Purpose

Individual data sheet: This provides students with an opportunity to understand the problem and attempt to solve the problem so that they have ideas to contribute to the group conversation. It allows for the method to be collaborative and to help build student capacity to participate in mathematical discourse.

Group data sheet: This element provides a vehicle for collaboration, on-task conversation, sharing of ideas, learning to value and consider the ideas of others, and attempting to reach consensus on a solution. The focus is not on the correct solution but on the ideas generated and the discussion focused on those ideas. The main purpose is to engage students in conversation around mathematical ideas in a somewhat risk-free situation.

Visit: This engaging component allows students to see and hear the ideas of other student groups and also provides a chance for them to consider the validity of their own solutions. The visit is not a social occasion, even though it feels like that to students. It is an opportunity to test out their solution several times and then return to their group and make a final decision about the solution. The process feels risk free, but it generates wonderful student thinking as they begin the process of learning to justify their solutions to problems.

Written explanation: Students are not typically accustomed to writing in mathematics, especially if they are not generally asked to explain their reasoning when solving a problem. The purpose of the written explanation component is to build students' capacity for explaining their reasoning. Writing in mathematics in a collaborative setting provides support for this skill, which is vital to good problem solving.

Circle discussion: This is a nice tool to use to create student engagement and involvement in mathematical discourse through the defense of a solution, but it is definitely not a presentation device. The overall purpose of the circle discussion is to provide students with the experience of making a final decision on a solution, deciding how they would justify that solution to others mathematically, practicing that defense, and then joining in a conversation with the whole class about their ideas. Throughout the process of the circle discussion, students are constantly deciding if they agree or disagree with the ideas of other student groups and why they have made those decisions. It's a great experience for students involving various levels of reasoning in a risk-free situation.

Teacher description of the solution: The main purpose of this component is to provide the students with the feedback of the solution after all of their hard work. But this feedback is done quickly by using a group data sheet (poster) from one of the student groups to explain the solution mathematically. This component is not meant to be a fully developed lesson delivered by the teacher based on the mathematical concept in the problem. It is very effective to use student work to present either a great idea for the correct solution or a common misconception that led to an incorrect solution. A solution explained based on the thought process of the teacher isn't as effective as utilizing student work to explain the solution.

Poster Method with Write-Up

This second method adds an independent product to the poster method in the form of an individual student write-up. The write-up focuses on an explanation of the solution and how it was developed and also on verification of the solution. In this method, at the conclusion of the poster method steps, before the solution is explained and revealed by the teacher, each student is asked to complete a two-part student write-up that includes a section on how their group arrived at the solution and if the student agrees or disagrees with that solution, and a second section in which the students explain why they think the solution is correct mathematically. The poster method sequence, write-up form, and feedback form are available in Appendix D.

The training for the poster method with a write-up is the same as the training for the poster method, with the addition of training students to complete a written explanation independently. The students will have had experience with creating a written explanation in a collaborative situation from using the poster method, so the extra training here will need to emphasize doing a written explanation independently. This means helping students become better at adding details to their writing and also including mathematical language in their descriptions. Students will also need to feel that their thoughts are valuable and worth writing down.

The Alternative Method

This method has several unique features that facilitate students developing an independent problem-solving product that shows evidence of student thinking and application of mathematical concepts to a contextual situation. The alternative method is collaborative, supportive, and engaging, but also allows students the opportunity to demonstrate their talents in the area of problem solving. It features working in triads, rotation to other groups, and a hint process that has been modified from the practice of using mathematical tasks to introduce concepts. The final product is partially developed in the collaborative setting in class and is finalized independently.

Training for the Alternative Method

It is recommended that the alternative method be used only after students have experienced at least the poster method, so it is assumed that students have already had training in collaboration, mathematical discourse, and written explanation. Additional training for this method includes:

Hint training: The hint process involves students going up to the front of the class and writing a hint on the board and explaining the hint to the class. Then each group has to decide if the hint is valuable to them in terms of solving the problem. The teacher doesn't make any comments about the hint. Students need to know the definition of a hint, how the process will work, and what the signal will be to indicate hint time during problem solving.

Summary writing: The alternative method is the only method described here that requires that students summarize individual work, collaborative work, their final solu-tion, and the mathematical justification of that solution. Students will need to know specific expectations related to the written summary and will also need some practice with writing such a summary, depending on their previous experience with expository writing.

Rotation: It is a good idea to practice the student rotation from one group to an-other before actually using the alternative method with a live problem. Students have to have clear expectations about how it works and where they go, and then the rotation is typically not a problem. Younger students may need a little more structure, but they quickly catch on to the process. The rotation works best if the group size is kept to three.

Recording collaborative work: Students need to be trained on how to use the write-up guide that goes with the alternative method. (The alternative method sequence, write-up form, and feedback form are available in Appendix E.) Each part of the write-up guide is designed to ensure that students are recording their thoughts as they progress through the problem-solving process and that they have a document to refer to when completing the final product for the method, which is the independent summary. Stu-dents need to be made aware of each section of the write-up guide and the directions and purpose of each section.

Sequence for the Alternative Method

Preparation

1. Select an appropriate problem.

2. Assign students to small cooperative groups of three.

3. Distribute the problem and an alternative write-up guide.

4. Have students count off (students number themselves one, two, or three within each group).

5. Have students create a data sheet.

6. Explain the "hint" process to students.

Solve the Problem

7. Let students attempt to solve the problem independently (five minutes).

8. Have students record their independent work.

9. Begin initial group work (10–12 minutes).

10. Have students record the initial group work.

11. Do the first rotation (students numbered "one" rotate to new groups).

12. Begin work with the second group (10–12 minutes).

13. Have students record the second group's new information.

14. Do the second rotation (students numbered "two" rotate to new groups).

15. Begin work with the third group (10–12 minutes).

16. Have students record the third group's new information (Note: The "hint" process introduced in step number six is ongoing during group work.)

17. Ask students to complete the "answer and verification" section of the write-up guide.

18. Create the final product independently (homework).

19. Process the solution (the next day in class).

20. Assess the completed student work (peer, self, and teacher evaluations).

Components of the Alternative Method and Their Purpose

Individual time: For this method, the purpose of individual time is to allow each student time to read and begin to understand the problem and the demands of the problem.

Rotation: This component is very interesting to watch in action. It provides students with a chance to gather different perspectives on the problem, to be exposed to possible strategies to reach a solution, and to provide support to other students who feel stuck. The rotation also has the effect of spreading information across the classroom environment, and actually adds to the positive energy and belief in efficacy in the room. The rotation combined with the hint process, is very supportive for students and helps them become proficient problem solvers.

Hint process: This process was modeled after instructional practices in problem-based classrooms that encourage student ideas to be shared while students are struggling with a worthwhile task focused on the topic for instruction before formal instruction begins. The reason for the inclusion of the hint process in the alternative method is to provide another level of support to students in the problem-solving process that is completely student centered and that provides students with the opportunity to evaluate new information in terms of the context, their understanding of the mathematics, and the more difficult task of making that evaluation in a collaborative setting.

Writing: The alternative method involves the students in written explanation at each step of the process to allow them the opportunity to enhance their metacognitive skills but also to improve their ability to describe in writing a collaborative problem-solving process. The other benefit of including writing in a problem-solving process is the improved student understanding of math terminology that results from it. As they work with the math concepts within the context of the problem, they are describing that work using the vocabulary from the unit of study that matches the problem-solving task.

Summary: This component is unique to the alternative method, and it offers students the opportunity to evaluate all the information that they heard in the different groups they were part of in the process and also the information from the hints offered by their peers, and make a final decision about the solution to the problem. The summary is built into this method as the independent portion of the method, but notice it is independent after much collaborative support has been provided.

Verification/justification: The idea of justifying or proving a solution mathematically is one of the goals of the alternative method. This method asks students to go to a higher level of reasoning and not only find a solution, but find a way to show how that solution is mathematically correct using their knowledge of the concept.

Sequence for Implementation of a Problem-Solving Program

Kindergarten

- Problem solving in kindergarten is a whole-class event based on word problems that involve a context that is engaging to the students and includes the use of the names of the students from the class in the problem. Students should work with a partner and have manipulative tools available to model solutions.

First Grade

- Begin like kindergarten at the beginning of the year if necessary, depending on your students.

- Start using the poster method.

- Eventually move to using the poster method with a write-up that is completed independently.

Second Grade

- Use the poster method.
- Move to using the poster method with a write-up that is completed independently by each student.

Third Grade to High School Courses

- The poster method
- The poster method with a write-up
- The alternative method

The goal is to have students involved in the alternative method as much as possible, but not to rush the process. You'll know when students are ready to move on to more formalized problem solving when they are confident, willing to stay with a problem and not give up, and have made good progress with explaining their reasoning to others verbally and in written form.

The Impact of a School-Wide Program

Creating a school-wide commitment to problem solving by all parties involved produces the best situation for students in their pursuit of understanding mathematics. If every grade that they move into emphasizes problem solving, the students not only gain confidence with thinking and reasoning and their own mathematical ability, but also they begin to think that math is a subject that is useful, engaging, and makes sense. This student belief in their own efficacy results in higher performance for the school population on math assessments.

Creating a Rubric, or Scoring Guide, for Problem Solving

Creating a scoring guide, or rubric, for problem solving will become essential once students start producing an independent product. The discussion that takes place among teachers to develop the scoring guide helps make the grading of student problem-solving products less subjective and creates a better feedback process for students.

It works best to develop a scoring guide in a collaborative setting. The conversation between educators helps clarify student expectations for the problem-solving process and in the end makes the grading process much more valuable for all concerned. The following process can be used to create a problem-solving scoring guide for a grade level, for a school, or for a school district. The more consistent the expectations for problem solving become, the better the students will perform, because they will understand what they need to do from one grade level to the next.

Sample problem solving rubrics are available in Appendix F.

Suggested Steps

- Teachers think individually about elements they would want to see in a student write-up for problem solving.

- In a collaborative group, teachers decide on elements that should be addressed in the scoring guide (correct answer, incorrect answer but correct process, math vocabulary, language mechanics, following directions, etc.).

- In a collaborative group, teachers define a proficient performance using the agreed-upon elements.

- Then teachers define levels above and below a proficient performance.

- Teachers field-test the scoring guide with a problem-solving activity, and adjust it as necessary.

Involving Students in the Process

A very interesting and beneficial option is to involve students in the process of developing a scoring guide for problem solving after they have done the poster method several times. The teacher provides the elements that will be used for the scoring guide and then students in small groups are asked to define a proficient performance and the levels above and below proficiency. The final step is to have a class discussion about the levels and make a final decision as to what will be acceptable to the students and the teacher as a description of the various levels of a student write-up in problem solving. The benefit of this process is student engagement in the assessment process and increased quality of student products because of students' complete understanding of the expectations. More information about how to include students in the development of rubrics is available in *Student Generated Rubrics* (1998) by Larry Ainsworth and Jan Christinson.

Criteria for Problem Selection

The process of selecting a problem-solving task for the methods that have been described is based on considering a few basic criteria.

- The problem should be related to the current unit of instruction and should allow students to show application of the mathematical concepts that are the focus of the unit.

- The level of difficulty of the problem depends on where your class is in the problem-solving process. If your students are in the "capacity building stage" (the poster method), then the level of difficulty needs to be on the easier side of the continuum to maintain student confidence and belief in their own efficacy. Students who have developed proficient problem-solving habits and who have experienced success with mathematical reasoning should be presented with more challenging problem-solving tasks.

- The problem-solving task should challenge mathematical reasoning by offering a problem situation in an engaging context that can be solved in various ways.

- From the standpoint of implementation, the most critical criterion for selecting a problem-solving task is that the classroom teacher understands the mathematics being applied in the problem, the various ways the problem can be solved, possible student misconceptions, and strategies that can be used to justify the solution for the problem.

Web Sources for Problem-Solving Tasks

- www.nrich.maths.org

- Noycefdn.org

- Mathforum.org (paid)

- www.fi.edu/school/math2/index.html

Variations for Early Grades

Kindergarten Problem Solving

Kindergarten problem solving is a group process using word problems based on a context that is engaging to students. The problems involve number sense themes that reflect current instruction and should utilize the students' names.

Problem solving at the kindergarten level is doing word problems that have unknowns at different places in the problem. This practice provides kindergarten students with valuable experience using the number sense patterns they are learning about within a context that is engaging and makes sense to them.

Here is a fun way to develop problems: Find something that all the kids are interested in, like a certain food or a current game or toy or television program. Then pick some student names from your class. Use the number sense pattern that is currently the focus of your instruction for the story (for example, doubles, one more than, making tens, etc.). Then use all those elements to create word problems.

For example: My grandson, Grayson, loves Mickey Mouse and he likes to eat the little crackers called Goldfish®, and let's say I've been practicing doubles with him. I could use the following problem to enhance and develop his problem-solving skills: Grayson and his friend went to Disneyland and saw Mickey. The first time they saw Mickey, he ate four Goldfish®. The next time Grayson and his friend saw Mickey, he ate double the number of Goldfish®. They saw Mickey one more time, and Mickey ate two more Goldfish®. How many Goldfish® did Grayson and his friend see Mickey eat?

Problem solving at the kindergarten level is a whole-group process so it really isn't the poster method, but it prepares kids for the poster method in first grade. The goal for problem solving at the kindergarten level is to give the students a chance to use what they have been learning and to give them essential practice with explaining what they are thinking about quantities within a context. Of course, the benefit of problem solving is that students see that math makes sense.

The sequence for problem solving in kindergarten is:

1. Read the problem together two or three times.

2. Have students think about and try the problem by themselves for three or four minutes.

3. Students work with their partner to try and solve the problem (they should have manipulatives to use to solve with), recording on a small whiteboard.

4. Whole-class discussion: students share different ideas they tried.

5. Whole-class solution: class and teacher solve the problem together using concrete objects.

6. Whole-class explanation: Create a few sentences that explain how to solve the problem by using input from the students. Write these sentences on chart paper and post them in the classroom.

This process should be fun and is a chance to honor student thinking.

First-Grade Problem Solving

First-grade students can do the poster method with the following variation of the process: Everything proceeds as described until the circle discussion. The circle discussion for first grade is a sharing process in which each group presents their ideas to the class. Then the teacher and the students solve the problem together using some of the students' ideas. This last step provides timely feedback to the students and also honors their mathematical reasoning and ideas.

Second-Grade Problem Solving

Second-grade students can do all the parts of the poster method. A helpful variation, initially, is to do the written explanation together as a class after the circle discussion to provide a model for written explanation in mathematics to the students. Doing this process a few times in second grade will help the students understand how to explain their reasoning and how to explain the steps they took to solve a problem. The major goals for problem solving in second grade are to build capacity and confidence in thinking and reasoning in mathematics for students as they move into the upper elementary grades and to provide beginning experience with written explanation in a problem-solving situation. Problem solving also helps second graders see that math makes sense and that it is useful.

Supporting Problem Solving on a Daily Basis

There are several things that can be done instructionally on a daily basis to support the problem-solving process and, more importantly, to support the reasoning and thinking that are fundamental to the application of mathematical concepts to problem-based situations.

Here are a few suggestions that are easy to implement and that will move your classroom instruction toward the mathematical practices required by the Common Core:

Questioning: Ask questions that require student thinking and reasoning as opposed to just asking for an answer. (What mathematical property matches this step? How are these ideas connected? What pattern do you see? Can a rule be developed from the pattern?)

Verification of solution: This idea is easy to put into the math review process daily and also into daily practice activities. Students are asked to state a mathematical reason for a step within a procedure or to show a model that justifies a solution. Small groups can be asked to discuss reasons to support solutions.

Using tasks or activities that allow for student struggle within instruction: This idea is a little more risky to implement but very valuable diagnostically for the teacher and very motivating and engaging for students. Problem situations or tasks that match the topic of the current unit are given to students prior to direct instruction on a skill or concept. The problems or tasks typically allow for generalization from a pattern or development of conclusions from information generated, so that when the time comes for formal instruction, students have already been allowed to struggle with the ideas that will be presented in direct instruction for the unit.

Modification of teacher questioning style: This is easy to implement, but it might mean changing some long-standing habits. The basic idea is to pay attention as a teacher to how long you wait before calling on a student after asking a question. Wait time is very powerful, because it allows everyone a chance to think about the question, but also causes all students to feel that they should think about the question. A good practice is to ask a question and then count to 10 in your head before calling on someone. To make it even better and raise the level of engagement, try not to call on individuals until you have allowed everyone not only some individual think time, but also some additional time to discuss the question with a partner. What that sequence does is engages the entire class, but also allows all students a chance to respond and paraphrase information, rather than one person being called on and everyone else feeling that they are off the hook for that question.

Writing in math on a regular basis: Writing in any content area is beneficial to thinking, and in mathematics it gives students the opportunity to make some sense of concepts that can be very abstract and difficult to learn. Writing allows the brain to clarify and construct meaning out of information that has been received. In the math classroom, students can be involved in daily reflection after feedback in the math review process, paraphrasing definitions of math terminology, paraphrasing information given within a lesson, and reflective processes after any lesson or feedback on homework.

Balance of teacher talk and student talk: Successful student problem solving is dependent upon students' ability to explain their reasoning and also their comfort level with speaking in class and sharing their ideas. If the math classroom environment is dominated by the teacher's voice, many students will be reluctant to attempt problem solving at all, especially the metacognitive elements of the process that feel risky to begin with. A beginning step to make the classroom more student centered is to pay attention to how much teacher talk there is compared to how much student talk there is, and try to make that at least a 50/50 situation. Then, over time, change the classroom environment so that there is more student talk than teacher talk. Try to honor student thinking and reasoning on a daily basis and provide for situations that will allow for their thinking to be shared and honored by the class. Always keep in mind that students don't learn math from just sitting and listening to an adult; they need to interact with the ideas and with each other to make sense of the concepts.

CHAPTER 3

A Balanced Unit of Instruction

In the conclusion of the opening chapter of *Visible Learning for Teachers* (2012), John Hattie discusses what "powerful, passionate, accomplished teachers" focus on to "make a sustained improvement" in student achievement. He found that they (p. 19):

- Focus on students' cognitive engagement with the content of what it is that is being taught

- Focus on developing a way of thinking and reasoning that emphasizes problem solving and teaching strategies relating to the content that they wish students to learn

- Focus on imparting new knowledge and understanding, and then monitor how students gain fluency and appreciation in this new knowledge

- Focus on providing feedback in an appropriate and timely manner to help students to attain the worthwhile goals of the lesson

- Seek feedback about their effect on the progress and proficiency of *all* of their students

- Have a deep understanding about how we learn

- Focus on seeing learning through the eyes of the students ... providing feedback about their errors and misdirections...

The unit design process described in this chapter has the necessary components to allow a teacher to focus on the elements of sustained student achievement mentioned in John Hattie's work. Each of the unit components will be described in detail from the viewpoint of how the process would be implemented into the curriculum planning procedure in a school or district.

When considering implementation of unit design in the area of mathematics, either at the school level for grade-level teams to use to organize instruction, or at the district level for curriculum development, several issues will need to be addressed. The two that I find are critical are the idea of "covering a textbook" and teachers' knowledge about the benefits of the "backwards design" approach to unit planning.

In my experience, it still is prevalent that teachers feel compelled to cover a textbook in mathematics to feel that they have done a good job for their students. The balanced unit design process presented in this section gives teachers a wonderful opportunity to be in the driver's seat when it comes to the planning process for the instruction and assessment that happen in their math classrooms.

The issue of "covering" material means the teacher, because of various pressures either internal or external, is teaching the curriculum without considering how students learn mathematics and how the human brain reacts to being exposed to information that is not attached to meaning or understanding. "Covering" is often connected to a textbook, which creates a situation where teachers are trying to cover a certain number of chapters and rely on the textbook series for many assessment and instructional decisions that should be made by the classroom teacher.

According to Grant Wiggins and Jay McTighe (2005), "one of the best ways in which to maximize learning is to use the notion of backward design." Backwards design is an important component in developing a balanced unit of instruction. Teachers who use backwards design find that they:

- Know where they are going instructionally
- Know what learning is essential in the standards
- Can use Big Ideas or Essential Understandings as a filter to determine instructional activities
- Become the instructional decision maker for their students
- Develop increased content knowledge and knowledge of the standards
- Focus instruction on essential understanding

John Hattie also discusses the benefits to teachers and students of knowing "learning goals" in *Visible Learning for Teachers* (2012). "The more transparent the teacher makes the learning goals, the more likely the student is to engage in the work needed to make the goal. Also, the more the student is aware of the criteria for success, the more the student can see and appreciate the specific actions that are needed to attain these criteria" (pp. 46–47).

A balanced instructional unit process driven by standards and the essential learning within those standards will allow teachers to meet the expectations of the Common

Core State Standards, which expect student understanding and higher levels of reasoning, problem solving, and various forms of assessment.

The following are steps to designing a balanced unit of instruction. (Unit design templates are available in Appendix G.)

Step 1: Identify a Grade-Level or Course Topic

This process is based on organizing instruction around mathematical topics and interrelated ideas to that topic, as opposed to covering a chapter in a textbook. The Common Core State Standards are organized to facilitate such a process.

Step 2: Find and "Unwrap" Relevant State Standards

This step anchors the process to the standards for the grade level or course. After standards are found that are related to the topic, those standards are "unwrapped," concepts and skills are listed, and cognition levels are listed. The "unwrapping" process is a method to determine the concepts and skills within a standard and to determine the level of reasoning expected within the standard. This process is described completely in *Rigorous Curriculum Design* (2010) by Larry Ainsworth.

Step 3: Develop Big Ideas

Writing Big Ideas for math standards isn't an easy process, and takes some practice. Because mathematics has been taught procedurally for several decades in the United States, many who teach math do not feel confident about identifying the conceptual understanding or essential understanding content within a grade-level standard for mathematics.

It is always best to find the Big Ideas connected to a math topic in a collaborative setting if possible. Start by answering the following questions about the selected topic.

- What is the concept connected with the topic?
- What are the difficult parts of teaching the concept?
- What are the important parts of teaching the concept?
- What are the errors and confusions that students tend to have when learning this topic?

• What are common student misconceptions? What could have caused these misconceptions instructionally?

After discussing the answers to these questions, it's time to move on to the knowledge package process. Liping Ma's classic work *Knowing and Teaching Elementary Mathematics* (1999) introduces the idea of a knowledge package. She explains how teachers in China used the concept when planning lessons for their curriculum in all subject areas. Their approach is to look at how ideas within a subject area are interconnected and to use that connection in their planning process for instructional units and individual lessons. I adapted the process to help with the development of Big Ideas in mathematics.

The Knowledge Package Process

This is an informal, associative process that is enhanced by conversation.

First, place the name of the topic in a circle in the center of a sheet of paper.

Teachers should ask, "What does a student need to know to be proficient with this topic?" Using the information generated from the questions at the beginning of Step 3, start to place ideas in circles as branches off of the main topic circle (see examples in Figure 3.1). Add as many ideas as come to mind. The number of ideas doesn't matter, but the more you have, the better, because of the connections they help create in your mind.

What you have created is a knowledge package for the topic that you are focusing on for instruction. The next step is to move into the realm of student misconceptions, which will typically lead you to the essential understanding, or Big Idea, that you are trying to develop. Look at your knowledge package and ask, "Where do students tend to have the most trouble?" or "Where do they develop the most misconceptions?" Then ask, "What is causing these misconceptions?" and "What is the essential understanding that students need so that they won't develop misconceptions?" From this information, the knowledge package can be prioritized to find the Big Ideas.

Using the information listed in the knowledge package, develop Big Ideas, or statements of mathematical understanding that fit the topic of the unit, and match them to the "unwrapped" standards.

This is not an easy process, but it is the most important piece of the unit design process because it sets the learning targets for the unit and is essential to developing the unit assessment. This is also the element that develops teacher clarity as to where the teacher is headed instructionally, and it is the element that, when shared with students, clearly lets them know what they are expected to understand and how they are expected to demonstrate that understanding.

FIGURE 3.1 Knowledge Packages with Related Big Ideas and Matching Essential Questions

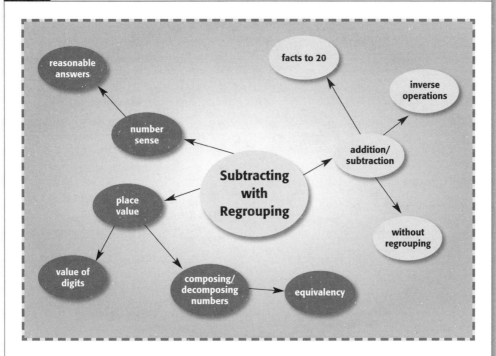

1. **Essential Question:** What happens if a quantity is rearranged?
   Big Idea: A given quantity can be arranged in different ways and the quantity is not changed.

2. **Essential Question**: How does the place value system work?
   Big Idea: The place value system is based on groups of 10.

3. **Essential Question:** What is the relationship between addition and subtraction?
   Big Idea: Addition and subtraction are inverse operations.

FIGURE 3.1 **Knowledge Packages with Related Big Ideas and Matching Essential Questions** *(continued)*

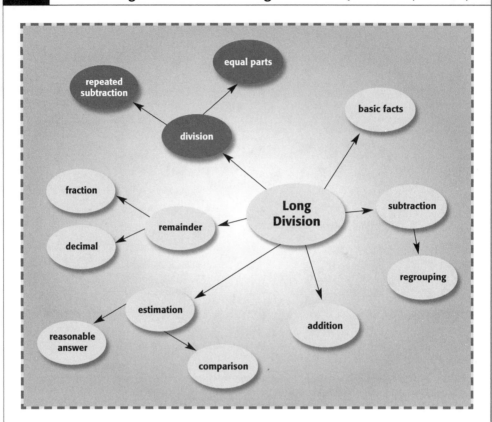

1. **Essential Question:** What is division?
   Big Idea: Division indicates how many equal groups are in a given quantity.

2. **Essential Question:** What is a remainder and how is it used?
   Big Idea: A remainder is a fractional part of the divisor that is used based on the context of the problem.

3. **Essential Question:** How can division problems be solved?
   Big Idea: Division problems can be solved using estimation, comparison, and reasonable answer.

FIGURE 3.1	Knowledge Packages with Related Big Ideas and Matching Essential Questions *(continued)*

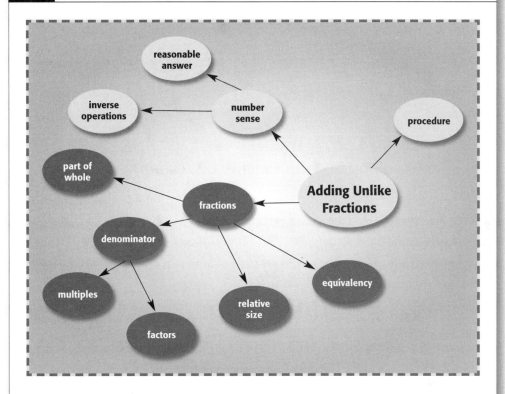

1. **Essential Question:** Why do you need a common denominator to add fractions?
   Big Idea: A common denominator is necessary so that you are combining same-size pieces.

2. **Essential Question:** How do you compare fractions?
   Big Idea: The relative size of a fraction is determined by the relationship between the numerator and the denominator.

3. **Essential Question:** What are equivalent fractions?
   Big Idea: Equivalent fractions label a given quantity that is less than one using different part-whole relationships.

Teachers need to be patient with this process and realize that it takes experience, and that it will be frustrating at first because it is a different way of thinking that they may not be used to.

The *Essential Understanding* series published by the National Council of Teachers of Mathematics (www.nctm.org/catalog/productsview.aspx?id=129) is a very helpful resource for this process, and *Elementary and Middle School Mathematics: Teaching Developmentally* (2010), by John Van de Walle and his colleagues, opens each chapter with Big Ideas that fit the concepts for the topic of the chapter.

Step 4: Write Essential Questions

An Essential Question is a question that matches the Big Idea and leads students to discover the Big Idea (which is the answer to the Essential Question). Each Big Idea should have a matching Essential Question. The Essential Questions are shared with students and can be used effectively as a pre-test for the unit and as part of the final assessment.

Step 5: Develop the Assessment and Rubric

An effective assessment will produce the evidence necessary to show student understanding of the Big Ideas for the unit. It also gives students the opportunity to demonstrate proficiency, as defined by a scoring guide, with the Big Ideas. An effective assessment is directly aligned to the Big Ideas and matches and informs instruction.

The most compelling reason for developing the unit assessment before the beginning of instruction is teacher clarity, which leads to student clarity. Other reasons are that the assessment can then guide instruction, can allow for constant references back to the Big Ideas during instruction to improve the clarity of students' understanding of what is expected, and it can enhance the feedback process for formative and summative assessment attached to the unit.

An effective, balanced assessment needs to have a variety of assessment item types to collect the necessary evidence of student learning. In mathematics, focusing on an answer to a problem will not provide sufficient evidence of student learning to fulfill the expectations of the Common Core State Standards or to deal with student misconceptions. The assessment items need to be designed so that students can show evidence of their reasoning and thinking, evidence of how they reached their solutions, and evidence justifying their solutions. Another critical criterion for assessment items is that they need to match the level of reasoning expected in the standards.

Here is a practical step-by-step process that can be used to build an assessment:

1. Arrange the test by Big Ideas.

2. For the first Big Idea, write four multiple-choice assessment items, two constructed-response items (students have to explain their reasoning), and two "show your work" problems in which students show all the steps they took mathematically to reach a solution.

3. For the remaining Big Ideas, follow the same process.

4. Then, for each item that requires written explanations or showing work, develop a statement of proficiency that specifically states what needs to be included in an answer in order for a student to demonstrate proficiency.

5. Next, create an answer sheet with the correct solution for each item and the necessary statements of proficiency included.

Writing good assessments takes practice and usually requires feedback in the form of field testing.

An excellent author to read for information about assessment is James Popham. One of his best books on this subject is *Test Better, Teach Better* (2003), which can be very beneficial when starting the process of becoming a good assessment writer for your students.

Optional Step:
Use Problem-Based Tasks to Introduce Big Ideas

This optional step is a way to start changing classroom instruction to match the expectations of the Common Core State Standards in Mathematics, and more specifically a way to infuse the Standards for Mathematical Practice into your unit instructional activities.

The idea is to use problem-based tasks to introduce each Big Idea before direct instruction begins for that Big Idea. Providing this opportunity to students allows them to struggle with the essential mathematical understanding within the Big Idea using their own math background, and provides valuable diagnostic information to the teacher about students' misconceptions.

To provide the teacher with valid and useful diagnostic information, the problem or activity that is used to introduce the Big Idea needs to be what John Van de Walle and other authors call a "worthwhile task."

A worthwhile task is defined as "any task or activity for which students have no pre-scribed or memorized rules or methods, nor is there a perception by students that there is a correct solution method" (Hiebert, et al., 1997).

Features of a Worthwhile Task
(Van de Walle, Karp, and Bay-Williams, 2010)

- It must begin where the students are.
- The problematic or engaging aspect of the problem must be due to the mathematics that the students are to learn.
- It must require justification and explanation for answers and methods.
- The result of the student work needs to be a product that will facilitate conversation or mathematical discourse.
- Problems may be posed for individual students, pairs, or groups.

Benefits of Meaningful Tasks
(Van de Walle, Karp, and Bay-Williams, 2010)

- They place the focus of attention on ideas and sense-making rather than on following the directions of the teacher.
- They develop the belief in students that they are capable of doing mathematics and that mathematics makes sense.
- They allow entry points for a wide range of students.
- They engage students so that there are fewer discipline problems.
- They are a lot of fun, for both teachers and students.

Development of Meaningful Tasks
As you begin to design a problem-solving task, consider these questions:

- What concepts will the task lead to? What concepts will students discover?
- What questions will be part of the task?
- What questions will be asked during instruction or processing?

Tips for Designing and Selecting Tasks

- Change textbook lessons into problem-based tasks matched to Big Ideas or essential understandings.

• Add a written explanation component to a traditional textbook lesson.

• The Navigating Series by NCTM is a wonderful resource for this option.

Example of Tasks and Big Ideas (Geometry Unit—Middle School)

Geometry Unit—Big Ideas

• Area is a measure of covering expressed in square units.

• Volume is a measure of capacity expressed in cubic units.

• There is a proportional relationship between perimeter, area, and volume.

Geometry Task—Area

• Determine the number of rectangles that can be made with 24 square units, then with 36 square units.

• Determine the area and perimeter for each rectangle.

• Create a chart for your results.

• Explain two ways to find the area of a rectangle.

• Explain the relationship between area and perimeter.

Geometry Task—Volume

• What determines the volume of a rectangular solid?

• Find two or more ways to determine volume.

• What happens to the volume if one dimension is doubled?

• What happens to the volume if two dimensions are doubled?

• What happens to the volume if three dimensions are doubled?

• Create a chart and diagrams to support your conclusions.

Both tasks are done in groups of four. Students used graph paper and square tiles for the area activity, and when it was time in the unit to do the volume task, they used unifix cubes to build rectangular solids. Each individual student made a product that answered the questions, but what was processed in class was the group product. The students in each group made a poster and some type of presentation to defend their answers. The "circle discussion" from the poster method of problem solving was used to facilitate class discussion.

Step 6:
Plan Instructional Activities Related to Big Ideas

Using the Big Ideas and the unit assessment as your guide, develop daily instructional activities that will facilitate student understanding of the mathematics included in the Big Ideas. Use whatever resources are available to you, including math textbooks, published math support materials, and online information. Of course, this is best accomplished in a collaborative manner if at all possible.

Step 7:
Select Problem-Solving Tasks Matched to Big Ideas

This step aligns the unit of instruction to the problem solving that was described in Chapter 2 and also makes sure that all the mathematical practices that take place in the problem-solving methods described become part of the instruction for the unit. At least two problem-solving tasks should be selected, and they should be matched to the Big Ideas for that unit. Including problem solving matched to Big Ideas for each unit gives students the opportunity to apply the mathematics that they are learning in the unit. The problem-solving tasks selected need to align to the Big Ideas for the unit and should be placed in the unit sequence so that students have the capacity to solve the problem.

Step 8:
List a Math Review Category Matched to the Unit Topic

As the math review process becomes efficient and students have internalized the procedures, it usually becomes easy to add a category that is specific to the current unit of instruction. I just called the category "conceptual unit." The idea is to think of typical misconceptions that students have with the topic of the unit and list those ideas so that they can be included in the conceptual unit category of math review during the unit. If you feel that math review is not efficiently operating when you do your first unit, you may decide not to include this step, but at some point it is a valuable process to students.

Step 9:
List Mental Math Themes to Support Big Ideas

The mental math process described in Chapter 1 is a great tool to use to build student capacity with number sense concepts and vocabulary concepts that are related to the current unit of instruction. While planning the unit, think of the number sense concepts or skills that often cause problems for students. Then provide daily practice with these concepts or skills by using the mental math process. You can even start before the unit instruction begins to give students an added sense of confidence.

For example: Say the next unit is about subtraction with regrouping. Mental math themes that will support that topic are 10 more than a quantity and 10 less than a quantity. Another supportive theme would be to practice with the value of digits in a number. If the next unit for instruction is about long division, which many students struggle with, a very supportive theme would be to practice daily with "how many equal groups are in a given quantity" problems so that division is not tied to the long division algorithm. In middle school, if your unit is about special triangles, in particular the Pythagorean theorem, a very supportive mental math theme is to provide practice with square numbers and square roots.

Step 10:
List and Plan to Teach Key Vocabulary

Students need to learn correct mathematical terminology to do well with mathematics instruction. A lack of understanding or even exposure to the language of mathematics has become a problem for many students at all levels of education across the United States. The issue shows up when students take assessments, when they are asked to solve problems, and especially when they are trying to make sense of a valuable subject called mathematics. Students of all ages can learn to "speak math." If they are exposed to made-up terminology, incorrect terminology, inconsistent terminology, or terminology that has nothing at all to do with the mathematics, it is not only detrimental to the student, but also very confusing to them as they search for understanding of the concepts they are expected to learn.

When designing a balanced unit of instruction, it is imperative that the key vocabulary words are listed and that a plan to teach those vocabulary words is included in the unit plan for instruction. A good example of a plan to teach vocabulary in a meaningful way is included in Marzano's book *Building Background Knowledge for Academic Achievement* (2004). I have found the process to be very effective at various grade levels. The vocabulary plan should also speak to when students can use the vocabulary in class. For instance, there are daily opportunities in math review and mental math to use vocabulary, and the problem-solving methods presented in Chapter 2 are based on student conversation and are full of opportunities to "speak math" correctly. A sample math vocabulary development activity is available in Appendix I.

Benefits of the Balanced Instructional Unit Design Process

- Provides a structure for instruction

- Creates a better understanding of standards for teachers and students

- Creates clarity of expectation for students and teachers

- Creates a situation in which instruction is not dependent upon a textbook and is not driven by coverage of chapters; the goal is student proficiency with essential ideas that are directly connected to math standards

- Allows teachers to decide how to teach concepts and what resources to use, and allows them to focus on the needs of their current students

- Facilitates common formative assessment and the Data Teams process, which leads to conversations about effectiveness of instruction at grade levels and across grade spans

- Results in improved understanding of assessment and improved use of assessments and assessment data

An Implementation Story—East Central BOCES

East Central Board of Cooperative Educational Services is located in Limon, a small town on the eastern plains of Colorado. The educational support organization supports 21 school districts of various sizes across an area more than 200 miles wide that ranges from the Denver airport to the Kansas state border. The BOCES is run by a small staff of wonderful, dedicated, hardworking educators who were willing to take on the task of designing and implementing balanced units of instruction based on the Common Core State Standards before the State of Colorado had made any final decisions about the Common Core or the assessment consortium that they would join. The story of East Central BOCES' curriculum team provides a model of how balanced units of instruction can be designed utilizing a team approach and the impact that approach can have on the educators involved in the process.

Curriculum Committee Approach to Develop Units of Instruction

The BOCES region had not worked on a math curriculum for the area in several years. As we were developing a math leadership team, we decided to also address the curriculum issue by developing a curriculum team for the region that would consist of grade-level representation from districts across the BOCES that were willing to participate in such a challenging project.

The curriculum team was established with at least two teachers for each grade level representing several districts in the region. In general, the approach taken was to train the educators in a section of the unit design process, and then have them try that part of unit design. The challenge was that the State of Colorado had not made a final decision about the Common Core State Standards or about the state assessment that was currently in use. The team was able to weather that storm, and become very effective at designing balanced units of instruction. The curriculum team followed this process:

- Examine the standards

- Learn how to "unwrap" the standards

- Learn how to develop Big Ideas and Essential Questions

- Make a format decision for the units for the region

- Goal: Develop Big Ideas and Essential Questions for the grade-level standards

- Become familiar with the 2009 Colorado state math standards

- "Unwrap" the standards

- Develop the Big Ideas and Essential Questions

- Develop the units of instruction

- Develop a suggested sequence for the units

- Decide how to provide implementation information to teachers

After Colorado decided to go with the Common Core, more guidelines were followed:

- Establish four key topics for each grade level

- Topics should reflect essential math concepts for the grade level

- Cross-reference Common Core State Standards to make sure the topic is included in that grade level; also check level of understanding

• Topics will be used for teacher training opportunities, lesson study activities, and video conference activities

We then tackled the idea of quality control and field testing of the units. Quality control was placed into the process after the initial training of the components of developing a unit. The curriculum team met at the BOCES office several days per year so that I could provide training and support. During our sessions, when a grade-level team would finish a portion of a unit I would meet with them to provide feedback and indicate what needed to be revised. We used that type of quality control as their expertise developed, then we moved to a sign-up process where a team would sign up to meet with me when they finished a unit with all the essential components so that I could provide feedback and they could do the necessary revisions.

The next step was very exciting for the BOCES region. The curriculum team combined with the math leadership team that had been established and set up a field-testing process for the completed units to get feedback from various school districts and to make sure that we were creating a useful product. The second component of the field-testing process was named "collaborative conversations," and took place after the units had been tried with students. The "collaborative conversations" event brought together teachers who had field-tested the units and offered them an opportunity to have a structured conversation about the units to provide feedback to the curriculum team. (Sample unit feedback questions are available in Appendix H.) The other part of the day was a demonstration of how to use the unit assessment as a vehicle for conversation across the region with teachers at the same grade level in different districts.

The preparation for that day consisted of:

• Plan for field testing and implementation

• Each grade level looks at the completed units

• Edit the units: spelling, titles of activities, problems, formatting, clarity

• Check the answer keys

• Check the resource links within the units to make sure they work

• Make sure the units are user friendly

• Develop a time frame for use of the units by your grade-level team (others who want to be involved will have to agree to the time frame)

• Determine the window of time to give the unit assessment

• Determine the actual date to share results

- Provide the format for sharing data

- Discuss methods to share in the BOCES region

- Create questions for feedback, such as:

  ◦ Did the suggested resources match the focus of the unit?

  ◦ Did the problem-solving tasks work?

  ◦ Was the unit well aligned to the Big Ideas?

  ◦ What were your general impressions?

- Request suggestions for improvement

- Determine if the assessment provided sufficient evidence to show student proficiency

- Determine if there is a need for strategies for differentiation

The collaborative conversations went well and allowed the curriculum team to continue their work on the units of instruction. The team's most recent progress resulted in six completed units for each grade, all aligned to the Common Core State Standards. They have added multi-step problems to unit assessments to match released items from the Partnership for Assessment of Readiness for College and Careers (PARCC) assessment consortium. The units of instruction are available on the BOCES Web site to all districts in the region and the units are also connected to a Colorado-based Web site that offers more resources for the development of individual lessons.

Keeping the curriculum team together and building their capacity for curriculum writing automatically increases the quality of the units that are produced and provides the BOCES region with a valuable resource. The level of expertise of the team members is amazing. They have increased their knowledge of assessment practices and their understanding of the connection between standards and instruction. As the Common Core State Standards are implemented and assessed in Colorado, the curriculum team members' expertise will become invaluable.

CHAPTER 4

Basic Math Facts

The issue of how to enable students to remember basic math facts is commonplace in school districts across the United States. Lots of blame is passed around to all parties involved as to why students fall short of expectations in this area, and much of what is done in the classroom is based on tradition rather than on information about how humans learn or memorize facts. Basically, it is not a good situation and it seems to be getting worse. The Common Core State Standards have provided some much-needed assistance by emphasizing number sense development in kindergarten through second grade, but the standards also expect fluency with basic math facts by the end of third grade. So something has to change.

Much of the problem stems from terms and phrases such as automaticity, fluency, timed testing, and "just memorize." If you take a look at the definition of some of these terms and compare that to information about how our brains learn, you'll start to see where the problem is coming from. Mathematical fluency is defined as using the math facts that you know to find the math facts that you are not sure of. Automaticity means that you can recall math facts in a timely fashion, which to educators means fast, but there isn't agreement as to how fast is fast enough. The fluency definition indicates some reasoning is going on, but the automaticity definition implies that you just know all the facts without thinking. Let's add in "just memorize," which indicates that if you practice enough, your brain will hold onto all the basic facts and that you can come up with the answers automatically (and quickly). That sounds good, but let's look at how the brain memorizes information and what makes the brain efficient.

In *Brain Rules* (2008), John Medina talks about the brain and learning: "Most people believe that the brain is a lot like a recording device—that learning is something akin to pushing the 'record' button (and remembering is simply pushing 'playback'). Wrong. In the real world of the brain . . . nothing could be further from the truth" (p. 104). Also, consider the impact of meaning on how the brain operates. "Information is remembered best when it is elaborate, meaningful, and contextual" (p. 114). So the traditional plan to "just memorize" the facts doesn't fit very well with what is known about how the human brain operates in a learning situation, especially if you want those facts to stay in long-term memory.

Just to cloud the issue a little more, consider the idea of timed testing and the use of timed testing as an instructional tool. A very common approach to teaching math facts in elementary grades in the United States is to have students do daily timed tests or to be involved in a commercially produced program that promotes the same approach. The first consideration is that timed testing might be fine for assessment but it isn't instruction. The main consideration is that a timed situation creates stress for students, which lowers the efficiency of the brain, especially in the situation of new learning. Basically, the timed testing isn't instruction at all, it's not a good practice situation, and considering what stress does to the operation of the brain, for most students the daily timed tests aren't teaching them anything except that they can't do math quickly enough.

You can see why there is a problem with mastery of math facts. An ideal math fact program will have an instructional component and an assessment component and will be based on the fluency model of learning math facts. According to Gina Kling (2011), "a fluency approach to learning basic facts places a focus on developing and using mathematical strategies, with the goal of finding efficient, effective ways to apply known facts to derive unknown facts."

The Fluency Model

- Develops number sense

- Enhances reasoning and understanding

- Increases students' belief in their own efficacy

- Allows students to demonstrate effective thinking strategies that involve decomposition and recomposition of numbers

- Develops more advanced student mathematical understanding

- Increases the likelihood that if students forget a fact, they will have a way to find it

Necessary Number Sense Information

There are a number of number sense patterns that enable a student to develop fluency with basic math facts.

Addition and Subtraction Patterns

- Commutative property of addition
- Doubles
- Combinations of 10
- Make 10 strategies
- One more/two more
- Facts with zero
- Near doubles ($6 + 7 = 6 + 6 + 1 = 13$)
- Subtraction—think addition, build up through 10 ($13 - 9$, $15 - 8$)

Multiplication and Division Patterns

- Doubles
- Fives
- Zeros and ones
- Nines
- Helping facts (3×8 is connected to 2×8—doubles plus 8 more)
- Multiplication before division
- Division's connection to multiplication

Building an Effective Math Fact Program

The creation of a math fact program should be completed with grade-level representatives for a school or for a district. It generally takes two or three days of work. The initial stage of the process involves making some difficult decisions, so it's important that there is administrative participation.

Goals of the Process

- Create an effective school-wide or district-wide math fact program that contains all the necessary components
- Create a math fact program that can be effectively implemented and sustained
- Create a program that all teachers will implement so that effectiveness can be determined

Components of the Program

- Grade-level expectations
- Assessment program
- Instructional program
- Remediation
- Record keeping
- Parental involvement
- Measuring program effectiveness
- Implementation plan

Before starting on the first component, it is important to have an open discussion about the issues listed below so that there can be agreement as to what instructional approach will be taken. Teachers will need an opportunity to examine what they believe about how students learn math facts and where timed testing belongs in the program (if anywhere).

Issues to Discuss Before Designing the Program

- How do students learn math facts and retain math facts?
- What is automaticity? What is fluency?
- What are the impacts of the two approaches—"just memorize" and "develop fluency"?
- What does current brain research tell us about memory?
- What is the tradition in the district or school regarding math facts?
- What is the level of parent involvement?
- What are the state expectations?
- Is number sense being taught in grades K–3?
- Do teachers know what number sense means and how to teach it?

After reaching some agreement about the critical issues involved with student learning and mastery of math facts, the committee of teachers should start with the first component—grade-level expectations.

Grade-Level Expectations

Designing this component involves each grade-level group making a decision about which math facts they should be responsible for in the math fact program. Teachers need to look at state math standards, Common Core expectations, and local expectations to determine what their grade level should be responsible for. The next step is essential: the committee has to get a sense of how students in the school or district are doing with basic math facts. Using this information, the committee will create grade-level expectations that may be a compromise from the expectations set in the standards so that some progress can be made toward more students becoming proficient.

For example, the Common Core State Standards expect fluency with the basic facts from all four operations by the end of third grade. Many districts or schools are currently not even close to that expectation, so when they are creating their grade-level expectations, they would have to keep that situation in mind. It is important to take students from where they are and build success, so that the math fact program that you build is successful from the beginning and creates a belief in efficacy toward mathematics.

It's important in this process that all grade levels agree to the final determination of grade-level expectations because all the other program components are dependent upon this decision.

Assessment Program

Before the committee can make any other decisions about assessment, they will have to have a discussion about the issue of timed assessments. Timing has been added to math fact assessment for various reasons, including the concern that students will use their fingers if there is no time constraint, that students don't really know the facts unless they produce them quickly, and the idea of automaticity. These and other reasons for timing math facts tests may have nothing to do with valid theories of learning and assessment. Also, the amount of time that different teachers or math fact programs consider to be fast enough varies considerably.

It turns out to be a very subjective process that has a tremendous impact on students and their feelings about math in general. An engaging issue to add to this discussion is the impact that a time constraint has on adults when they are asked to perform in different situations. The reality is that most adults don't do well with time constraints in assessment situations. It can be very valuable to discuss that we know that time constraints place stress on the brain, which lowers the efficiency of the brain, and we know that most adults don't do well with time constraints on assessments, so why are we assuming that timed testing is a valid situation for kids?

It can also be enlightening to have the members of the committee take timed math fact tests at different rates to determine what a fair amount of time for a given number of problems might be. No matter how you go about your discussion, the committee needs to make the following decisions:

- Will your program use timed testing for assessment?

- If the program uses timed testing for assessment, how much time will be given for how many problems?

- Will the timing and number of problems change depending on grade level?

- What happens to students who can't handle timed testing? What alternate form of assessment will be available?

The assessment component and instruction component go hand in hand, so many times when making assessment decisions the committee will have to examine what they intend to do instructionally. The next step is for the grade-level teams to start making decisions about assessment design and then the committee as a whole will discuss the decisions and come to agreement for consistency.

Decisions to Be Made about Assessment Design

- What are the grade-level expectations for fact mastery (sequence of facts)?

- What will be the assessments for the grade level, including partial assessments as facts are being learned, and a final assessment for the grade level (mixed facts)?

- What are the recommendations for the timing element of assessments and for alternative assessment procedures for students who can't handle timed tests?

- What are the recommendations for proficiency levels?

Things to Consider When Making Final Decisions

- Assessment sheets—should they be organized by operation and subgroups or strategies within operations?

- Should operations be assessed separately and then together?

- Assessment sheets should allow for easy diagnostic information.

- Should there be a different format of assessment for different grade levels?

- How often should students be assessed? (Typically once a month or every six weeks.)

- Students must show grade-level proficiency until the end of the year for the math facts to stay in long-term memory.

- Alternative formats should be available for students who can't handle timed assessment.

- What should the level of proficiency be? (90 percent? 100 percent?)

- How will the results of the assessments be used? (What will happen next for students who are proficient? For students who are not proficient?)

Instructional Program

This is the component that will determine if the level of student math fact mastery in your school or district changes. An effective math fact program must have the two essential components of instruction and assessment, with the emphasis being placed on the instruction. If your school's or district's current math fact program has consisted of daily math fact timed tests, which is currently very common, that means it has been missing the instructional component. In other words, students have received lots of assessment without the matching instruction. The instruction needs to be based on number sense development, allow lots of practice, and hopefully be a daily process.

One of the key issues to decide will be when the math fact instruction will take place. Will it happen daily? How long will it last? How will it be structured? Then, a basic plan for instruction must be developed.

Susan O'Connell and John SanGiovanni, in their book *Mastering the Basic Math Facts in Addition and Subtraction* (2011a), organize instruction around Big Ideas about our number system. For example:

- Our number system is a system of patterns.

- The order of the factors does not change the sum.

- Addition and subtraction are inverse operations.

- Numbers are flexible. They can be broken apart to more easily perform an operation.

John Van de Walle and colleagues' approach (2010) is number sense based and allows students time to find comfortable and reliable strategies for fact retrieval. Their recommendations for teaching math facts include:

- Develop strong understanding of operations and number relationships

- Develop efficient strategies for fact retrieval

- Provide drill with efficient strategies

Resources

The following three resources are the best I have found for helping teachers with organizing math fact instruction around number sense concepts. All three resources fit the fluency model of instruction.

- *Elementary and Middle School Mathematics* (2010), by John Van de Walle, Karen S. Karp, and Jennifer M. Bay-Williams

- *Mastering the Basic Math Facts in Addition and Subtraction* and *Mastering the Basic Math Facts in Multiplication and Division* (2011a and 2011b), by Susan O'Connell and John SanGiovanni

- *Number Sense Routines* (2011), by Jessica Shumway

Methods to Support Math Fact Instruction

Use of math review: The math review process that was described in Chapter 1 can be very useful as a support for math fact instruction and practice. Teachers can include a math fact category on math review called a "survival box." A math fact is placed in the survival box and students are asked to write two ways that they could find the answer to the math fact if they didn't know the math fact. Those different ways are shared out in class when the math review is processed. (For example, 7×8 would be placed in the survival box. Students might say, I could find 7×8 by using 7×7 and adding 7 more, or I could use 8×10 and subtract 8×3.) Math review is also a great place to emphasize the idea of reasonable answer with students on a daily basis, which is foundational for their sense of quantity.

Use of mental math: The mental math process as described in Chapter 1 is a perfect match for math fact practice. Use themes that emphasize basic fact patterns to provide daily practice for students in a risk-free manner that provides positive feedback. Staying with a theme for at least two weeks gives students the opportunity to find fact retrieval strategies that are comfortable and reliable for them.

Lessons within units on operations: Choral response within algorithm instruction.

Practice activities: Board games, teacher-made games, flash card games, centers in the classroom, whole-class games—any activity that allows for mental practice of basic facts and has elements of feedback, fun, and engagement is great practice for basic facts.

Specific instruction about number properties: Students should be specifically taught about the properties of the number system that make learning math facts easier, such as the commutative properties of addition and multiplication and the properties of one and zero. This type of instruction helps students see that there aren't as many facts to learn as it seems.

Remediation

As the math fact program is implemented, over time students who struggle will be identified. It is recommended that a math fact program include a plan for students who need special assistance with math fact mastery and number sense development. This type of plan needs to be developed by considering what resources are available at the individual school level to offer regular assistance to students who are struggling. The most effective resource for this situation if at all possible is people—teachers, instructional coaches, parent volunteers, etc.

Record Keeping

Record keeping for the math fact program is essential to determine if the instructional component is working and also to give a realistic picture of how students are doing with math fact mastery at a classroom, school, or district level. The record-keeping component also gives students feedback as to how they are progressing with the task of learning basic math facts. The design of the record-keeping system should match current resources and the assessment culture of your school district.

An important criterion to consider is that the individual student records need to follow the students from kindergarten through fifth grade so that each teacher starts the year knowing the math fact status of each student in class. The students also need to start the year with that information so they can develop their individual goals for math fact mastery. Most schools are finding that this type of record keeping can easily be accomplished electronically using a spreadsheet approach.

An example of record keeping is available in Appendix P.

Parental Involvement

Parents can be a very valuable resource in the quest to improve student fluency with basic math facts. Involving parents in a positive way brings math into the family setting using a topic that parents and students can have some fun with if they are provided with some guidance.

Hosting "family math nights" for various grade levels can be a very effective tool to provide parents with education about math facts and math in general, and also to create wonderful enthusiasm around what your school is doing with mathematics instruction to help students. The original resource for this idea, *Family Math* by Jean Kerr Stenmark, Virginia Thompson, and Ruth Cossey (1986), is still available. On the Internet, there are many resources available, including videos, PowerPoint presentations, and books that explain in detail how to host a family math night for any grade level.

Other ways to effectively include parents in this goal include using parent volunteers to support student practice and alternate forms of assessment and providing math fact instructional and practice information to parents at back-to-school nights or curriculum nights.

Measuring Program Effectiveness

When implementing a new math fact program that has several components, it is necessary to develop a plan to determine effectiveness so that adjustments can be made as needed and also to keep track of the different components and their impact on student learning. A plan for measuring program effectiveness will typically need to involve a building-level administrator or district-level leadership.

The plan should address the following questions:

- How will effectiveness be determined?
- What data will be used?
- How will grade-level effectiveness be determined?
- How will school-wide effectiveness be determined?
- How will necessary adjustments be made?
- Who will monitor the program?
- How will changes be made?

Implementation Plan

The implementation plan will vary depending on whether the program is for a school or for a district. For either level, the main concern will be providing training in how to teach number sense and how to teach math facts, not just assess math facts. If prior to developing a math fact program teachers were just using timed testing for instruction, then it is critical that training and resources be provided on how to teach number sense and math facts within the fluency model to enable teachers to maintain fidelity to the instructional component of the math fact program. Without support and training for the instructional component, it is likely that little change in student success will be experienced.

The following questions should be used to develop an implementation plan at the school level or district level:

- How will the math fact program be shared with all schools or all grade levels?

- Who will provide the necessary training? What will the training consist of?

- Who will provide follow-up training and feedback to teachers who are participating?

- Should the math fact program be district- or site-based?

Middle School Level

Many districts find that math facts are still a problem for middle school students, so when they develop a math fact program they include the middle level grades in the plan for the first few years to do what they can about student gaps and to create as much student success as possible. The approach in middle school is focused on helping those middle school students who think they don't know any math facts to realize that they *do* know quite a few math facts and that they can learn to use what they know to figure out what they don't know. In other words, the emphasis for middle school students has to be a fluency model of math fact mastery and not more of the same timed testing without number sense instruction that they experienced in grade school.

The first step for a student that gets to middle school and still does not know basic math facts is to point out to them the math facts that they *do* know. Then help them develop a plan to learn key facts that will help them figure out everything else using the fluency model. The next step for these students is critical. They have to start experiencing success with math facts so that they stop resisting the entire idea and so that they start building some belief in their efficacy toward number sense in general. Most students who feel they can't do math facts by the time they get to middle school have also decided that they are not "math people." They have equated their inability to pass timed math fact tests that haven't been supported by instruction with their cognitive ability to do math. Nothing could be further from the truth, but it is a difficult attitude to change when students are at the middle school age.

If students can experience some success with math facts; if they are shown that they actually do know some math facts; if they are shown that there are wonderful patterns in the number system that actually make sense and that can be used to figure out answers that they have not memorized; if they realize that they do mental calculations just like other students and that they have a natural capacity to do that, these middle school kids will put forth effort toward improving their math fact fluency. But again, if all they receive is more of what they saw for the prior five years, it won't work. Middle school is typically the last chance to do anything formally about number sense and basic math fact fluency.

Here are some questions for discussion to guide the development of a middle school math fact program:

- Is there an assessment tool to determine which facts students know and which they do not know? Will the results be student friendly?

- How will you design a record-keeping system for the math fact gaps that students have?

- How will the students be instructed differently? What support will be provided? Can schedules be changed to provide support?

- How will student progress be determined?

An excellent example of the key components of a math fact program is included in Appendices J–Q. The example from Tempe Elementary School District includes a description of the math fact program, examples of instructional strategies to teach basic math facts, assessment and record-keeping examples for grade 2, and examples of how to include math review and mental math in the program.

CHAPTER 5

A Model for Instruction

Individual lessons within a unit of instruction in math should be structured in such a way that they satisfy the Common Core's Standards for Mathematical Practice, they help students become mathematically proficient, and they are consistent with how students learn. The fourth-grade fractions lesson presented in this chapter satisfies those requirements, and contains many of the components that should be in place in a math classroom to enhance student understanding of mathematical concepts and to build students' belief in their own efficacy in mathematics. The implementation of this suggested instructional model, along with math review, mental math, problem solving, balanced instructional units, and the development of a math facts program, will align a teacher's math instruction with what is expected by math standards such as those in the Common Core, but more importantly, it will align instruction with what is known about how students learn.

Three days of instruction taken from a unit on fractions in fourth grade will illustrate an effective model for instruction. The unit is based on the Common Core standards for fourth grade and on Big Ideas developed from the standards using the process described in Chapter 3.

The Classroom

In this fourth-grade classroom, students have been involved in math review and mental math on a daily basis. The students have also been doing the problem-solving methods described in Chapter 2, and have been receiving math fact instruction based on the fluency model described in Chapter 4. Students are adept at having on-task mathematical conversations and explaining their thinking to other students. They have also gained experience with writing in mathematics and with the idea of justifying their solutions to problems. The overall environment is one of collaboration—student thinking and student voice are valued, and there is not an overemphasis on teacher explanation.

This classroom is using a technique from Robert J. Marzano's *Building Background Knowledge for Academic Achievement* (2004) called an academic notebook that I modified for use in my math classes. Students have an individual "knowledge notebook" in class that they use for reflections in math class on Essential Questions, for vocabulary activities, and for personal reflections as they proceed through a unit of instruction.

Instructional Philosophy

• All students should receive grade-level content with the necessary support to become proficient.

• Students do not learn math by sitting and listening; they must be active participants in the learning process.

• Math instruction must be grounded in meaning. It has to make sense to students, or the mathematics will not be learned or remembered.

Common Core Standards for Unit

Grade level: Fourth grade

Topic for the Unit: Fractions

Common Core State Standard: 4.NF.2—Compare two fractions with different numerators and different denominators, e.g., by creating common denominators or numerators, or by comparing to a benchmark fraction such as 1/2. Recognize that comparisons are valid only when the two fractions refer to the same whole. Record the results of comparisons with symbols >, =, <, and justify the conclusions, e.g., by using a visual fraction model.

Fractions Learning Progression (Grades 3, 4, and 5)

The Common Core State Standards were developed using the idea of learning progressions for mathematical concepts. It is a good practice to look at the grade-level standards above and below the grade level that you are teaching to determine where the standard that you are working on fits within the learning progression. The standard for this series of lessons focuses on the comparison of fractions with unlike numerators or unlike denominators. Notice that the third-grade standard focused on comparison of fractions with the same numerator or the same denominator and that the fifth-grade standard adds in mixed numbers and the use of equivalent fractions. The idea is to make sure you know where your specific grade-level instruction fits in the learning progression.

Third grade (3.NF.3d)—Compare two fractions with the same numerator or the same denominator by reasoning about their size. Recognize that comparisons are valid only when the two fractions refer to the same whole. Record the results of comparisons with the symbols >, =, <, and justify the conclusions, e.g., by using a visual fraction model.

Fifth grade (5.NF.1)—Add and subtract fractions with unlike denominators (including mixed numbers) by replacing given fractions with equivalent fractions in such a way as to produce an equivalent sum or difference of fractions with like denominators.

Essential Questions and Big Ideas

• **Essential Question:** What determines the size of a fraction?
  Big Idea: The relative size of a fraction is determined by the relationship between the numerator and the denominator.

• **Essential Question:** How are fractions compared?
  Big Idea: The size of fractions can be compared using common denominators and by referencing benchmark fractions.

• **Essential Question:** Why is a common denominator necessary?
  Big Idea: A common denominator allows you to compare same-size pieces.

Lesson 1: Comparing Fractions

The first day of the unit and the first lesson of the unit will involve students in what John Van de Walle and his colleagues call a "problem-based task" (2010, p. 34) to introduce the first Big Idea of the unit. The Essential Question that matches the Big Idea is used in the task to directly connect the standards to instruction. The reason for completing a task with students before any direct teacher-driven instruction occurs is based on what Guershon Harel (2007) calls the "necessity principle." He says, "For students to learn what we intend to teach them, they must have a need for it, where 'need' refers to intellectual need, not social or economic need." Harel further states, "Many students, even those who are eager to succeed in school, feel intellectually aimless in mathematics classes because we (teachers) fail to help them realize an intellectual need for what we intend to teach them." He says the phrase intellectual need "refers to a behavior that manifests itself internally with learners when they encounter an intrinsic problem."

Each Big Idea for the unit will be introduced by using a problem-based task to create intellectual need for the students, to allow them to struggle with the mathematical ideas before instruction, and to provide valuable diagnostic information to the teacher before starting direct instruction. This approach is used in problem-based programs and is very common in countries such as Singapore that are very successful mathematically (National Center for Education Statistics, 2011).

Sequence for the lesson:

• Students are placed in groups of four.

• Students individually answer the Essential Question—How do you compare fractions?—in their knowledge notebooks.

• Students share their thoughts about the Essential Question with group members.

• Students remain in groups of four. The fraction task is explained to the students:

  ○ Compare the following fractions according to size. Put them in order. 1/2; 1/4; 3/8; 2/4; 2/8; 5/8; 4/4; 6/8.

  ○ Use a model to show how your group decided the size of each fraction.

  ○ Display your order on a number line.

  ○ Write two statements about the size of a fraction and numerators and denominators.

  ○ Answer the Essential Question—How do you compare fractions?

  ○ Create a poster or other product that can be used to share your groups' answers.

  ○ Prepare for the circle discussion (the circle discussion is the same technique used in the poster method for problem solving described in Chapter 2). Remember that all group members need to participate in the circle discussion.

The expected outcome of this task is student discussion and the presentation of—and support of—student ideas. It provides the teacher with very enlightening information about the students' understanding of the topic. This activity is not an opportunity for the teacher to explain the correct answer or the correct method.

Lesson 2:
Direct Instruction Connected to the Fraction Task

Materials recommended: pattern blocks

Learning targets from the standard: common denominators, reference to 1/2

Sequence:

1. Have students discuss with partners what they found out from the task about comparing fractions.

2. Introduce pattern blocks and set guidelines for use of the materials.

3. Let students investigate the relationships demonstrated by the pattern blocks. Share with the whole class.

4. Using the pattern blocks, build equivalent fractions together. (The teacher builds using a document camera, student pairs build with the pattern blocks.)

5. Record on the board what fractions are equivalent each time. Have students record this information in their knowledge notebooks.
   - Hexagon (yellow piece) $1/1 = 1$
   - Trapezoid (red piece) $2/2 = 1$
   - Rhombus (blue piece) $3/3 = 1$
   - Equilateral triangle (green piece) $3/6 = 1/2$, or $6/6 = 1$, or $2/6 = 1/3$ (do all three, if there is time)

6. Write the following statement together (the teacher writes on the board, students write in their knowledge notebooks): "A common denominator allows you to compare same-size pieces."

7. Have students discuss with their partners what they think the statement means. If there is time, have students talk with two or three other students.

8. Have students build the following with pattern blocks:
   - 1 (hexagon)
   - 2/3 (rhombus)
   - 1/2 (trapezoid)

9. Make sure students notice that they can tell the relative size of these three fractions just by looking at the models. Tell them that mathematics has another way to compare fractions using same-size pieces.

10. Tell the students that now they will build some equivalent fractions that can show relative size.

11. They will build equivalent fractions by covering up the pieces they just had used with equilateral triangles (green pieces).
    - 1 (hexagon) = 6/6
    - 2/3 (rhombus) = 4/6
    - 1/2 (trapezoid) = 3/6

12. Make sure students notice that the numerator indicates which fraction is larger or smaller, because of the same-size pieces, and that they can tell the pieces are the same size because the numbers in the denominator are the same.

13. Next, reference the idea of the benchmark fraction 1/2. Have students notice that a good way to start to decide the size of fractions is to compare the fraction to a benchmark fraction like 1/2. Have them try the idea with the three fractions they have been working with.

Independent practice:

Have students work with their designated partner.
Students will use the fractions from the fraction task on the first day for independent practice. This is also an effective way to provide meaningful feedback.
- Task: Compare the following fractions according to size. Put them in order. 1/2; 1/4; 3/8; 2/4; 2/8; 5/8; 4/4; 6/8.
- Student directions: Use reference to 1/2 and common denominators to decide the relative size of the fractions.
- The students need to write down the statements of how they developed their solutions.
- When students are finished, provide feedback by building equivalent fractions, and drawing models.

Reflection:

Have students return to the Essential Question from the first day in their knowledge notebook and have them add to their response based on lesson two.

Homework:

Place the following fractions on a number line. Use common denominators and comparison to 1/2 to explain in writing why you are correct. 3/8; 1/4; 1/2; 6/8.

Lesson 3: Tangram Activity

This lesson is designed to increase the level of student reasoning and to take what was accomplished in direct instruction and let students practice the concepts in the context of a problem that involves struggle but has the element of immediate feedback. Students will need tangram sets, and they will work with designated partners.

The lesson begins with brief feedback on the homework using the math review feedback process that includes error analysis and reflection (described in Chapter 1). The remainder of the lesson is the tangram activity.

Sequence:

- Build the tangram together. Student pairs will start the task, and then the teacher will show the class the final construction so that students can proceed with the activity.
- With their partners, students label each piece with a fraction.
- Students make a list of equivalent pieces and label them with fractions.
- Students decide the common denominator that could be used to compare the pieces.

Feedback:

Use the student-directed approach from the math review model that is explained in Chapter 1. Partners are selected to share their solution and then ask the class if they agree or disagree with their solution.

Reflection:

How did you do with the activity? Write what you know about equivalent fractions and common denominators. Complete the reflection in your knowledge notebook.

Homework:

Practice of the same type of problems as in lesson two.

Key Components of the Model for Instruction

• Lessons consist of meaning-based instruction connected to Big Ideas.

• All lessons include student interaction, conversation, and metacognition.

• Direct instruction is included to provide correct mathematical information.

• Guided and independent practice are always matched with effective feedback and student reflection.

• The focus of the lessons is on essential understandings within the topic.

• The level of reasoning increases across the series of lessons.

• Student voice and teacher voice tend to be equal in the classroom environment.

• Lessons should not be dominated by teacher explanation.

• Students interact with the mathematical ideas during lessons.

• Written explanation is included as often as possible.

• Intellectual curiosity is established for students through the use of tasks.

• Instructional activities are engaging.

Connections with the Common Core and Mathematical Proficiency

Mathematical Proficiency Elements

(Necessary for a student to learn mathematics successfully)

Conceptual understanding (comprehension of mathematical concepts): In the lessons, relative size is taught through the use of models and referencing a benchmark fraction, a concept that should be in students' experience. The concept was not taught as a procedure without meaning.

Strategic competence (ability to problem solve): The lessons included two distinct problem-solving tasks.

Adaptive reasoning (capacity for reflection, explanation, and justification): These components are used throughout the three lessons.

Productive disposition (see math as sensible, useful, and worthwhile, coupled with a belief in diligence and one's own efficacy): The engaging design of the lessons, coupled with the development of intellectual curiosity and teaching with understanding, will lead students to believe in their own efficacy toward mathematics.

Common Core Standards for Mathematical Practice Elements

Problem solving: Problem-based tasks are used in the lessons.

Reason abstractly and quantitatively (to abstract a given situation and represent it symbolically and manipulate the representing symbols as if they had a life of their own): Students use pattern blocks to draw conclusions about the relative size of fractions.

Construct viable arguments (students justify their conclusions and communicate them to others): Each lesson involves student communication and justification of solution.

Attend to precision (students try to communicate precisely to others. In the elementary grades, students give carefully formulated explanations to each other): The design of each lesson has elements to allow students to use the language of mathematics in a contextual situation that supports that language. The lessons also facilitate the development of metacognitive skills by asking students to explain how they can justify their answers.

Time Management: Putting It All Together

- Sixty minutes per day for math instruction:
  - Math review—15 minutes
  - Mental math—three minutes
  - Homework feedback—seven minutes
  - Unit lesson—35 minutes
- Math review and mental math—daily
- Math review quiz—biweekly
- Formal problem solving—biweekly

CHAPTER 6

Models of Implementation

Implementation of a balanced math program can be accomplished in a wide variety of school situations and using multiple different approaches. As long as all the key elements are implemented with fidelity, a balanced approach to math instruction will improve student results in any school situation. This chapter illustrates this by describing the implementation of a balanced math program in two very different groups of schools, and concludes with a list of the key components of successful implementation.

Tempe Elementary School District No. 3

The Tempe Elementary School District is located in the heart of Arizona's "Valley of the Sun." It encompasses an area of approximately 36 square miles, including not only Tempe but also parts of Phoenix and the town of Guadalupe. The 20 schools in the Tempe Elementary School District consist of 14 elementary schools grades K–5, a developmental special needs school, three middle schools grades 6–8, a K–8 school, and a K–8 traditional school (a district term indicating a school that uses traditional teaching methods). The student population of Tempe Elementary School District No. 3 consists of diverse cultural, ethnic, and socioeconomic groups. There are approximately 12,000 students in the district.

The Tempe district had worked very hard for several years on language arts and reading education in particular to meet the needs of the large number of students in the district who are English language learners. The district found that they needed to do something about the structure of math instruction in general and also start preparing for the implementation of the Common Core State Standards.

The implementation process in Tempe Elementary School District was facilitated by Professional Development Coordinator Pam Stetka, and was completely supported by administrative leaders at all levels in the district.

Elements Implemented: Years 1 and 2

- Grades 3–8 cohort of teacher leaders was trained and supported.
- Kindergarten through grade 2 cohort of teacher leaders was trained and supported.
- All schools were visited to provide feedback to teacher leaders and other interested teachers.
- Follow-up trainings were provided based on visits to schools.
- Building principals attended all trainings for both cohorts.
- District-level administrators attended trainings for both cohorts.
- Started with grade 3–8 cohort, then in the second year developed K–2 cohort to support implementation of Common Core State Standards.
- Individual schools within the district were provided with additional support.
- Teacher leaders were provided with continuing support to share information with other staff members.

Elements Implemented: Year 3

- Instructional coaches were added to the process.
- Implementation of math review, mental math, and the developed math fact program was now the responsibility of the instructional coaches and building administrators.
- Training and support of instructional coaches became the priority.
- Instructional coaches were trained in math review and problem solving.
- Instructional coaches were trained in feedback and the coaching process.

Implementation Sequence

Year 1: 3–8 Cohort—math review, mental math

Summer between years 1 and 2: District math fact program developed

Year 2: K–2 Cohort—math review, mental math, trained for problem solving and began implementation; Grade 3–8 Cohort—math review, mental math, problem solving

Year 3: Both cohorts—maintain math review, mental math, and problem solving, and implement math fact program

Note: During all three years, the math leaders of the district were adjusting and developing units of instruction to adjust to the adoption of the Common Core State Standards.

Key reasons for success with implementation:

- Cohort approach; training and supporting teacher leaders that stayed with the implementation process
- There was administrative participation (including the superintendent) in all aspects of the process, including school visits and feedback sessions
- The district math leaders maintained fidelity to the processes that they were trained in

East Central BOCES

The East Central Board of Cooperative Educational Services (BOCES) is located in Limon, Colorado. The BOCES services 21 school districts with 9,400 students in grades pre-K–12 and 560 classrooms in a region that stretches from near the Denver airport to the Kansas border, covering nearly 15,000 square miles.

The community populations range from 35 to 4,000, with the school district enrollment sizes ranging from 60 to 3,000 students. Ranching and farming are the major economic contributors. School districts are experiencing declining enrollments on a continuing basis.

The East Central BOCES region had not done any consistent work on its mathematics program in several years. The challenge of this situation was that the leaders at the BOCES were attempting to support change in math instruction across 21 different districts, not just within one district. In the BOCES region, each of the 21 districts, no matter what size, has a superintendent, a school board, and principals. The BOCES structure provides no administrative authority. It is a service and support organization. We had to build the implementation plan knowing that if districts did not find the information useful, they would not show up.

The work with East Central BOCES started in 2009 as a three-day training on balanced instruction in mathematics, with implementation visits to schools and districts in the region to support the implementation process. The work became much more comprehensive due to the dedication of two wonderful educators, Sharon Daxton-Vorce, the Staff Development Coordinator for East Central BOCES, and Anita Burns, the Federal Programs Coordinator for East Central BOCES, and also due to an amazing group of tenacious teachers on the BOCES curriculum team. The teachers *did* show up in this plains region of Colorado (even though they didn't have to), and as of this writing they are still showing up and doing the good work.

Implementation Process

- Initial training in the balanced approach—plan to implement math review
- School and district visits to support implementation process and assess math programs
- Second training offered in balanced approach
- School and district visits
- Proposed long-term plan developed based on visits
- Math review categories developed, with more than 100 teachers representing districts in the region
- Long-term plan finalized—The overall structure to improve math instruction in East Central BOCES will consist of a leadership team with teacher and administrative representation from participating districts, and a curriculum team that will consist of grade-level teams of teachers and/or administrators.

Leadership Team Definition

- Participants—classroom teachers representing various grade levels from a school or district; building administrators; instructional coaches
- Objective—improve classroom instruction in mathematics by utilizing teacher leadership
- Goal—90 to 100 percent implementation and monitoring of trained strategies

Leadership Team Expectations

- Participate in initial training
- Implement trained strategy in classroom

- Participate in advanced training for strategy

- Continue to use trained strategy and collect student data

- Develop implementation plan with school or district administrator to share information with other teachers

- Share strategies with other teachers

- Provide support to other teachers as they implement strategies

- Communicate with school or district administrators

- Attend East Central BOCES leadership team support sessions

Support Provided to Leadership Team

- Initial training for the balanced approach

- Advanced training in different components

- School and classroom visits to provide feedback, model lessons, discuss issues with teaching staff, etc.

- Materials as needed

- East Central BOCES will provide the math review categories, units of instruction, and current information on Common Core standards and state testing

- E-mail, phone calls, conference calls

- Other members of leadership group

Curriculum Team Expectations

- Become familiar with standards (Colorado/Common Core)

- "Unwrap" standards

- Develop Big Ideas and Essential Questions

- Develop units of instruction

- Develop suggested sequence for units

- Develop implementation information for teachers

- Understand the benefits of the process and be prepared to share them with other teachers

- Be patient with yourself and with the process—there are different ways of thinking; it's a collaborative process; it influences instruction; it is not easy

Implementation Process After Teams Were Established

- Regular meetings for support and capacity building on selected topics for both teams

- School and district visits to support implementation of trained strategies

- VNET broadcasts by consultant to support development of teacher capacity; themes of the broadcasts were math review, mental math, problem solving, and instruction in math facts

- Units of instruction were developed and field-tested. A revision process is in place. A quality control process is in place. Units are aligned to the Common Core.

- Collaborative conversations—field testing

- Data collection process for the region was discussed and is in development stage

- Math review survey tests were developed and aligned to the Common Core with the help of both teams

- Technology to share developed units and materials has been developed

- Both teams meet throughout the year to monitor implementation and to be informed of new information impacting math instruction in the region.

Key Reasons for Success with Implementation

- Development of the implementation plan after the initial training and after visiting districts within the region

- The two-team approach (leadership and curriculum) to create a high level of involvement in a situation where the BOCES doesn't have any central authority for implementation

- Both teams had administrative and teacher participation

- Team members have been willing to stay together and stay with the process

- The curriculum team's capacity in the areas of assessment and instruction has grown tremendously

Key Components of Effective Implementation

Implementing change of instruction in mathematics is not an easy task. Change is not easy in any part of education, but for various reasons changing math instruction seems to meet with an extraordinary amount of resistance.

Teacher resistance comes from a lot of different sources. The ever-present "cover the material" model is responsible for a great deal of resistance. Teachers have convinced themselves that they must cover a textbook or cover a curriculum or course or their students won't be successful. The driving force in their classrooms is coverage of the material, not the teaching of students. A teacher with this mindset is very resistant to change in instruction because the strategy they are being asked to implement will get in the way of their goal to cover whatever it is they feel they have to cover. Once this type of teacher becomes more student centered instead of material centered, the resistance will lessen, but that isn't always an easy task.

Tradition in math education is another area of resistance. This is very common at the secondary level, because secondary math teachers typically understand mathematics quite well and can't imagine why anyone wouldn't be able to learn math the way they were taught. "I learned it that way when I was in school, why can't the kids now learn that way?" This type of teacher is usually the dominant voice in the classroom and relies upon "the telling method" of teaching math: I'll tell you how to do the problem from my perspective and how I understand it. You practice the problem the way I told you. Then we'll move on. That type of classroom has little student interaction or engagement and definitely almost no student voice except for the few students who are called upon. The first question for this type of teacher is to ask how students perceive their instruction, what all the students know after the instruction, and how the teacher knows how students perceive instruction and what they know. The traditional telling method won't allow the teacher to answer those questions. Again, this type of teacher has to become much more tuned in to student thinking, student misconception, how students learn mathematics, and the power of engagement.

The biggest obstacle to change in classroom practice is teacher comfort and risk. Many teachers will resist because they're not sure how this strategy could work and they are definitely convinced they cannot do it successfully. This obstacle is typically overcome with good support, effective feedback, and patience.

Resistance will be there, but if the following key components are in place, it can eventually be overcome. One of the best ways to overcome teacher resistance to a new way of teaching math is to provide evidence that when implemented with fidelity, the new system works better than the old one and results in higher rates of student success in your school or district. Teachers all over the country have improved student success in mathematics by successfully implementing math review, mental math, problem solving, and developing balanced units of instruction. Developing a plan that will result in early successes that can be celebrated and held up as proof that the new programs are working will help to quiet the naysayers.

Key Components for Successful Implementation

- Administrative support throughout the entire process
- Administrative knowledge of the process being implemented
- Observation and evaluation of current instructional practices, not just test scores
- Fidelity to key components of the strategy being implemented
- Classroom observations with effective feedback for all teachers implementing the process
- Training support and information support
- Collaborative model for all adult participants
- Focus on student learning
- Capacity building for teacher leaders
- Decisions about instruction must be data-driven

CHAPTER 7

The *Balancing Mathematics Instruction* DVD

The DVD included with this book is the result of tremendous work by a lot of wonderful people. This filming project was made possible by Pam Stetka and Amanda Gomez from the Tempe Elementary School District, Sharon Daxton-Vorce from the East Central BOCES, Kevin Skattum of the Light Group in Broomfield, Colorado, who directed the filming, and Katie Schellhorn Stoddard, formerly of The Leadership and Learning Center, who helped get this project off the ground. Of course, the real stars who made it possible to film classrooms in action are the students and teachers who put in the time and effort to implement these strategies over time and had the courage to change what they had been doing with mathematics instruction. The DVD's classroom segments, filmed in classrooms in Tempe Elementary School District in Tempe, Arizona, and Burlington School District in the East Central BOCES region of Colorado, show the impact on students and the classroom environment when strategies are implemented with fidelity. They also demonstrate that it is possible to have math instruction become engaging and student centered at all levels with all kinds of students. I think they are a joy to watch.

Contents

Section 1 of the DVD shows the author describing the components of the math review process with classroom clips to allow the viewer to see the components in action. Specifically, there is a segment on the teacher-directed method and a segment on the student-directed method. Section 1 also includes a segment on mental math, the poster method for problem solving, and the alternative method for problem solving.

Section 2 contains classroom segments that illustrate math review and problem-solving methods. The teacher-directed and student-directed methods are featured in the math review segments. The poster method and the alternative method are featured in the problem-solving segments.

The specific segments are:

- Math Review—Teacher Directed; Kindergarten; Katie Koehn; Thew Elementary, Tempe Elementary School District

- Math Review—Teacher Directed; First Grade; Alana Mohr; Frank Elementary, Tempe Elementary School District

- Math Review—Student Directed; First Grade; Katie Garcia; Nevitt Elementary, Tempe Elementary School District

- Math Review—Student Directed; Sixth Grade; Erika DeReinzo; Fees College Preparatory Middle School, Tempe Elementary School District

- Math Review—Student Directed; Eighth Grade; Kandi Young; Burlington Middle School, Burlington School District

- Problem Solving—Poster Method; Third Grade; Sonja Long; Aguilar Elementary, Tempe Elementary School District

- Problem Solving—Poster Method; Fifth Grade; JoAnn Madden-Crohn; Thew Elementary, Tempe Elementary School District

- Problem Solving—Alternative Method; Eighth Grade; Lindsay Palmer; Fees College Preparatory Middle School, Tempe Elementary School District

- Problem Solving—Alternative Method; Algebra I; Nikole Cox; Byers High School, Byers School District

Section 3 contains testimonials from administrators in the Tempe Elementary School District and districts within the East Central BOCES region that explain the impact of implementing balanced instruction on the teachers and students in their respective school districts.

Suggested Use

The DVD segments can be useful for the initial training of educators in each of the processes in *Balancing Mathematics Instruction*. This can be accomplished by having teachers view the DVD segments that are relevant to their grade level and that match the training that they have received. The DVD classroom segments and also the explanation segments provide teachers with a more complete picture of the methods so that they are more likely to implement them with fidelity. The DVD segments are also very effective within a feedback structure for teachers periodically throughout the implementation process.

Another use for the DVD segments is to build the capacity of math coaches to assist with the implementation process of the strategies defined in the balanced approach to math instruction. Coaches could watch a section of a segment on a given strategy and then have a discussion based on the following questions: Do you know the reason for that step? Do you know the research attached to this strategy? Do you know the impact on students of what you just watched? Do you know the key elements for implementation of this strategy? What questions do you expect from teachers, and do you have answers for those questions?

The DVD can also be used very effectively by an individual teacher to learn the strategies described in the book. Begin with the information in the chapter that describes the strategy you want to try. Then watch the segments that pertain to that information to bolster your understanding of the strategy. Try the strategy in your classroom and go back to the DVD segment and the feedback sheet provided in the resource chapter and see how it is going. Reflect on your progress and keep trying.

Appendices

Sample Key Ideas
for Math Review Categories

The category is listed first, followed by the key idea(s) for that category.

Expanded notation:
> The value of a digit is determined by its position.

Scientific notation:
> Powers of 10 move the decimal point.
> Scientific notation is used for very large or very small numbers.

Subtraction with regrouping:
> Numbers can be rearranged to help with subtraction.

Regrouping:
> A quantity can be rearranged in different ways and it is still the same quantity.

Multi-digit multiplication:
> Partial products can help determine an answer to a multiplication problem.
> The value of a digit is determined by its position.

Multiplying decimals:
> Multiplying the whole numbers helps place the decimal.
> A reasonable answer helps place the decimal.

Division:
> Division indicates the number of equal pieces in a given quantity.

Division with remainder:
> A remainder is part of the divisor expressed as a fraction or a decimal.

Adding unlike fractions:
> A common denominator shows same-size pieces.

Equivalent fractions:
> A fraction can be represented in various equivalent ways.

Telling time:

A clock uses a base of 60.

Each number on a clock represents groups of 5.

Telling time involves skip counting by 1s and 5s interchangeably.

Money:

Counting money involves skip counting by 1s, 5s, 10s, and 25s interchangeably.

Geometry:

Shapes are classified by their attributes.

Area is a measure of covering expressed in square units.

Perimeter is the distance around a shape expressed in linear units.

Area:

The area formula comes from the perpendicular relationship of base and height.

Algebra:

An equation shows two equivalent quantities.

Solving an equation involves undoing the order of operations.

Proportional reasoning:

A proportion is two equal ratios.

Integers:

Adding the opposite helps with subtracting integers.

Data:

Mean, median, and mode tell about the center of the data.

Math Review Process Scripts

TEACHER-DIRECTED METHOD

Students prepare their math review papers by writing their name and the date in the upper right corner and writing the title "Math Review" on the top line of the paper. Students are told that they need to number each problem, copy the problem on their paper, and show all of their work. Students repeat those directions to their partners.

Students work on the problems independently for two minutes.

Students work with their designated partners to finish the problems for six minutes.

At the end of eight minutes, students put away their pencils and take out their marking pens or pencils.

The teacher will now lead "teacher-directed" processing, which is a direct, specific, feedback system.

Teacher Dialog

Feedback for directions: "Star your name and date. If you didn't write one or the other, write it now with your marking pen."

"Star the title 'Math Review.' Write it now if you didn't. Look to see if you numbered the problems, copied the problems on your paper, and showed all your work. If you did all three, write on your paper that you are awesome at following directions. If you didn't do all three, write on your paper that you need to follow directions."

Feedback for problems—error analysis: The teacher indicates parts of the solution to the problem that should be starred if they are correct or circled and fixed if they are incorrect.

Students then write a one-sentence reflection based on the error analysis they completed for the problem.

The teacher says and writes the key statement for the problem. Students write the key statement on their paper and stand up when they are finished. Students say the key statement to their partner. The class says the key statement together.

The same process is followed for each problem.

STUDENT-DIRECTED METHOD

Students work on the problems with their partners for eight minutes.

During the student work time, the teacher circulates through the classroom and finds partners that are doing well on the problems and invites student partnerships to present the problems to the class.

At the end of the eight-minute work time, student-directed processing begins. The teacher stands in the back of the room and facilitates the process but allows the students to have the stage.

The student-directed method is an "agree/disagree" process that involves students providing feedback about the problems and asking the class if they agree or disagree with the information.

Student Dialog

Feedback for directions (provided by the first student pair): "Hold up your marking pen. Star your name and date. Tell your neighbor if you did this correctly. Star the title 'Math Review.' Check to see if the problems are numbered, the problems are copied, and all your work is shown. Write 'I'm awesome at following directions' on your paper if you did all three. Write 'I need to follow directions' if you didn't do all three. "

Feedback for problems—error analysis: One of the students begins the feedback process on the first problem. "Star the vocabulary word for the problem if you wrote it. If not, write it on your paper now." Then the students show, in a step-by-step process, what they think is the necessary work for the problem. After each step, they ask the class if they agree or disagree with the work they are showing. When agreement is reached on the correct work and solution, the presenting students ask the class to "star" what is correct and "circle and fix" what is incorrect.

The student presenters then lead the class through the reflection process and the key statement process using the same sequence as in the teacher-directed process.

A different set of student partners is selected for each problem.

Math Review Feedback Form

Teacher Name: _____ Date: _____

Classroom Environment

☐ Students are working with each other to complete the math review problems.

☐ Students are showing their work on their papers for each problem.

☐ Students have access to the prior day's math review paper.

Processing of Math Review Problems—Teacher-Directed Method (first three days of a new category)

☐ Teacher provides specific feedback for problems using error analysis (students star portions of the problem that they did correctly and circle and fix portions of the problem they did incorrectly).

☐ Students write a reflection about their performance for each problem based on the error analysis.

☐ Students write or say a "key statement" for each problem.

Student-Directed Method (after three days of teacher-directed)

☐ Student partners provide feedback to the class using error analysis just as the teacher did. The student partners are preselected during the time students are working.

☐ Students lead the class in the reflection and key idea statement process.

☐ Teacher facilitates the process from the back of the room.

Mental Math

☐ A mental math problem is a series of calculations that students do in their mind ($3 \times 5 - 7 + 8 = ?$).

☐ Mental math problems are based on number sense themes.

☐ Each problem is repeated twice.

☐ Students share reasoning to reach solutions.

☐ Mental math should be a daily process.

Problem Solving—Poster Method

POSTER METHOD SEQUENCE

1. Students should be in **groups of 3 or 4.**

2. Students each need an individual piece of paper that they will label "data sheet" and a pencil.

3. Explain to students what a **data sheet** is and how to use one. (*A data sheet is a place to record your thoughts about solving a problem. It doesn't matter if the ideas are correct or not. Write down anything that you try.*)

4. **Read the problem to the students. Read the problem with the students twice.**

5. Have the students try the problem individually for eight to 10 minutes.

6. Have students stop working and **write two complete sentences** on their individual data sheets about what they did to try to solve the problem. Students stand up when they are finished writing.

7. When all students are standing, have **two or three students read their sentences to the class**. Do not comment on the sentences. Simply say, *"Thank you for sharing."* These sentences provide information for all students to consider as they move into the collaborative part of this method.

8. Students **work in their groups to solve the problem** and try to reach agreement on a solution. It's fine if they can't agree. They can agree to disagree.

9. Provide students with poster paper and marking pens.

10. Students create a **group data sheet** that indicates the group's solution (or solutions if they can't agree) and ideas from each member of the group.

11. Before the group data sheets are complete, do the **"visit."** The "visit" involves one student remaining at their group's location to explain the ideas on the group data sheet. The remaining group members visit other groups to discuss their ideas about solving the problem (two to three minutes).

12. Everyone returns to their group. Each group has a brief discussion about the visit and makes a decision about their solution. Do they want to change their solution or stay with their solution?

13. Finalize group data sheets.

14. Have students complete the **written explanation** on the back of the group data sheet. Students answer the following questions in detail: How did your group solve the problem? How does your group know the answer is correct mathematically?

15. Provide rehearsal time for the "circle discussion" if necessary.

16. **Circle discussion**: All groups state their solution; have a group that is confident about their solution defend their solution; start the math discussion by asking which groups agree and which groups disagree. Call on groups to say why they agree or disagree. The teacher's role is to ask questions to keep the discussion going but not to comment on anything being stated by students.

17. Use a group data sheet to **explain the solution to the class.**

POSTER METHOD SUGGESTED WRITE-UP FORM

Name: _____ Date: _____

Title of the Problem: _____

What do you think the answer is to the problem? _____

How did your group solve the problem?
Explain in words. Use as much detail as you can remember.

_____

_____

_____

_____

_____

_____

Explain how you know that your answer is correct mathematically.

_____

_____

_____

_____

_____

_____

POSTER METHOD FEEDBACK FORM

Problem Selection

☐ The problem relates to the current unit of instruction.

☐ The problem is at the appropriate level of reasoning for the students.

☐ The problem is relevant and engaging to students.

Student Behaviors

☐ Students work independently for eight to 10 minutes.

☐ Students record their thinking on individual data sheets.

☐ All students are engaged in on-task group discussions and are working toward a solution.

☐ All students are actively engaged in developing the group data sheet.

☐ There is evidence of each member's contribution.

☐ During the "visit" students are engaged in mathematical discourse.

☐ During the "circle discussion" students are engaged in mathematical discourse.

Comments for Student and Teacher Behaviors

Teacher Behaviors

☐ Teacher strategically places students in groups of three or four to do problem solving.

☐ Teacher reviews process and expectations of individual data sheet.

☐ Teacher monitors students working without indication of accuracy or providing assistance to students.

☐ Teacher requires students to write two or more complete sentences about what they tried in solving the problem.

☐ Teacher asks two or three students to share sentences.

☐ The classroom environment is not answer-driven. Student reasoning, metacognitive practice, and written explanation are emphasized and celebrated.

☐ The teacher acts as a facilitator during the process and does not engage in instruction or directions for solving the problem.

☐ The teacher guides the "circle discussion" with appropriate questions that enhance student discussion.

☐ The teacher uses a group data sheet from one group to demonstrate the solution to the problem.

Problem Solving—
Alternative Method

ALTERNATIVE METHOD SEQUENCE

Preparation

1. Select an appropriate problem.
2. Assign students to small cooperative groups of three.
3. Distribute the problem and an alternative write-up guide.
4. Have students count off (students number themselves one, two, or three within each group).
5. Have students create a data sheet.
6. Explain the "hint" process to students.

Solve the Problem

7. Let students attempt to solve the problem independently (five minutes).
8. Have students record their independent work.
9. Begin initial group work (10–12 minutes).
10. Have students record the initial group work.
11. Do the first rotation (students numbered "one" rotate to new groups).
12. Begin work with the second group (10–12 minutes).
13. Have students record the second group's new information.
14. Do the second rotation (students numbered "two" rotate to new groups).
15. Begin work with the third group (10–12 minutes).
16. Have students record the third group's new information. (Note: The "hint" process introduced in step number six is ongoing during group work.)
17. Ask students to complete the "answer and verification" section of the write-up guide.
18. Create the final product independently (homework).
19. Process the solution (the next day in class).
20. Assess the completed student work (peer, self, and teacher evaluations).

ALTERNATIVE METHOD SUGGESTED WRITE-UP FORM

Title of the problem: _____

1. Individual work (record what you did to try to solve the problem by yourself):

2. Cooperative work (record what you did to try to solve the problem with others):

3. Answer and verification (write your answer and explain how you know your answer is correct mathematically). Use the back of the paper.

ALTERNATIVE METHOD FEEDBACK FORM

Problem Selection

☐ The problem relates to the current unit of instruction.

☐ The problem is at the appropriate level of reasoning for the students.

☐ The problem is relevant and engaging to students.

Student Behaviors

☐ Students work independently for three minutes.

☐ Students record thinking on their individual data sheets and then on the write-up guide.

☐ All students are engaged in on-task group discussions and are working toward a solution.

☐ Students offer hints in a risk-free environment.

☐ Students rotate to new groups and remain on task and engaged in each group.

☐ Students record group interactions on the write-up guide using complete sentences.

☐ Students create an individual write-up including verification of solution.

Comments for Student and Teacher Behaviors

Teacher Behaviors

☐ The teacher strategically places students in groups of three or four to do problem solving.

☐ The teacher reviews the process and expectations of individual data sheets, the write-up guide, and the hint process.

☐ The teacher requires students to write two or more complete sentences about what they tried in solving the problem after each group interaction.

☐ The classroom environment is not answer-driven. Student reasoning, metacognitive practice, mathematical discourse, and written explanation are emphasized and celebrated.

☐ The teacher acts as a facilitator during the process and does not engage in instruction or directions for solving the problem at any point during the solving portion of the process.

☐ The teacher uses student solutions and verification to develop the solution within a class discussion.

Problem-Solving Rubrics

PRIMARY GRADES

Name: _____ Title of problem: _____

Exemplary

☐ All "Proficient" criteria *plus*:

☐ Written work explains, step by step, the process used to solve the problem

Proficient

☐ Correct answer

☐ Solves problem on data sheet with words, pictures, and/or numbers

☐ Includes number sentence that matches problem

☐ Follows all problem-solving guide directions to complete write-up

Progressing

☐ Meets three of the "Proficient" criteria

Beginning

☐ Meets fewer than three of the "Proficient" criteria

☐ Task to be repeated after remediation

Self evaluation: I think my score is _____ because _____

Teacher's evaluation: This score is _____ because _____

Notes:

Proficiency must address the *mathematics*.

Students have ongoing opportunities to reflect upon and revise their work with feedback using the scoring guide.

UPPER ELEMENTARY GRADES

Name: _____ Title of problem: _____

Exemplary

☐ All "Proficient" criteria *plus*:

☐ Proves answer mathematically

☐ Written work explains why answer is correct

Proficient

☐ Correct answer

☐ Solves problem on data sheet using computation and/or graphic representation (words, pictures, and/or numbers)

☐ Written explanation matches data sheet

☐ Shows correct mathematical reasoning

☐ Uses math vocabulary appropriate to problem

☐ Follows all problem-solving guide directions to complete write-up

Progressing

☐ Meets four to five of the "Proficient" criteria

Beginning

☐ Meets fewer than four of the "Proficient" criteria

☐ Task to be repeated after remediation

Self evaluation: I think my score is _____ because _____

Peer evaluation: I think this score is _____ because _____

Teacher's evaluation: This score is _____ because _____

Notes:

Proficiency must address the *mathematics*.

Students have ongoing opportunities to reflect upon and revise their work with feedback using the scoring guide.

SECONDARY GRADES

Name: _____ Title of problem: _____

Exemplary

☐ All "Proficient" criteria *plus*:

☐ Verifies answer mathematically

☐ Written work explains verification of answer

Proficient

☐ Correct answer

☐ Solves problem on data sheet using computation and/or graphic representation

☐ Written explanation matches data sheet

☐ Shows correct mathematical reasoning

☐ Uses math vocabulary appropriate to problem

☐ Follows all problem-solving guide directions to complete write-up

Progressing

☐ Meets four to five of the "Proficient" criteria

Beginning

☐ Meets fewer than four of the "Proficient" criteria

☐ Task to be repeated after remediation

Self evaluation: I think my score is _____ because _____

Peer evaluation: I think this score is _____ because _____

Teacher's evaluation: This score is _____ because _____

Notes:

Proficiency must address the *mathematics.*

Students have ongoing opportunities to reflect upon and revise their work with feedback using the scoring guide.

Unit Design Templates

TEMPLATE ONE

Grade Level: _____

Topic: _____

Related Standards:

"Unwrapped" Skills and Concepts:

Big Ideas and Matching Essential Questions:

End-Of-Unit Assessment (include a mixture of selected-response items, constructed-response items, and performance task items):

Scoring Rubrics (statements of proficiency for each constructed-response and performance task item):

End-of-Unit Assessment Option (include Essential Questions as part of unit assessment; describe proficient answers for each Essential Question):

Problem-Based Instruction Option (develop one task for each Big Idea to begin instruction):

Instructional Activities Related to Big Ideas:

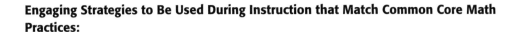

Engaging Strategies to Be Used During Instruction that Match Common Core Math Practices:

Action Research Option (linked to common formative assessment/Data Teams processes; list research-based strategy that team will use during instruction):

Two Problem-Solving Tasks that Match Unit Big Ideas (list names of problems and method to be used):

Math Review Category that Supports Unit:

Mental Math Themes that Support Unit:

Key Vocabulary and How the Vocabulary Will Be Taught:

TEMPLATE TWO (EAST CENTRAL BOCES)

Grade Level or Course:
Topic:
Related Standards—Colorado State and Common Core Standards (text):
"Unwrapped" Skills and Concepts/Key Vocabulary (link):

Big Ideas (text):	**Essential Questions (text):**
End-of-Unit Assessment (link):	**Unit Assessment Scoring Guide (link):**

Problem-Solving Tasks (link):
Suggested Activities to Build Understanding of Big Ideas (links):
Mental Math Themes (text):

Unit Feedback Questions

These feedback questions were developed by East Central BOCES.

Your name: _____

School: _____

Grade level: _____

Unit name: _____

    Number of students that participated in the unit: _____

    Length of time to teach the unit: _____

Today's date: _____

1. Were the Big Ideas and Essential Questions useful in developing your daily instruction?

    Yes   or   No

    Explain: _____

    _____

    _____

    _____

    _____

    _____

    _____

    _____

2. Were the suggested activities and resources useful in daily instruction?

    Yes   or   No

    Explain: _____

    _____

    _____

    _____

    _____

    _____

    _____

3. Were the suggested activities and resources that you used aligned to the Big Ideas and Essential Questions?

   Yes   or   No

4. Explain how you used the problem-solving tasks and what the student results were.

   _____

   _____

   _____

   _____

   _____

   _____

5. Does the unit assessment show quality evidence of student proficiency with the Big Ideas?

   Explain: _____

   _____

   _____

   _____

   _____

6. Briefly describe how your students performed on the unit assessment.

   _____

   _____

   _____

   _____

   _____

7. Reflect on your overall experience in teaching this unit.

   _____

   _____

   _____

   _____

   _____

   _____

Example of Math Vocabulary Development Activity

This activity was adapted from Robert Marzano's *Building Background Knowledge for Academic Achievement* (2004) and Larry Ainsworth and Jan Christinson's *Five Easy Steps to a Balanced Math Program* (2006).

Step 1: Students individually cluster what they know about the given topic, for example, "circles." After clustering, students share their clusters with a partner and add to their own clusters during the sharing process.

Step 2: The teacher presents to the class a teacher-made definition of each math word associated with the topic, and then repeats that definition. Students paraphrase the teacher's definition in writing and draw a graphic representation to match. After writing their paraphrased definitions, students discuss them with partners and revise if necessary. They then repeat the process for each of the words presented.

Step 3: Working in small groups of three or four, students create similes or metaphors for the vocabulary words and then share those with the class. Examples:

- A radius is like a spoke on a wheel.
- Circumference is a snake biting its tail.

Step 4: After they complete the metaphor and simile activity, students revise their paraphrased definitions in their academic notebooks.

Step 5: While in the same groups, students play a pantomime game. One member of the group is chosen to act out one of the circle words, and the other members of the group try to guess the word from the pantomimed clues.

Step 6: Without referring to their notes, students create a cluster to show all that they now know about circles. After doing this, they self-reflect by referring to the notes they took during the earlier steps.

Overview of Math Facts Strategies

These strategies are from Tempe Elementary School District.

Below is a list of strategies that are commonly used to solve unknown math facts. They are listed in a suggested order of introduction. As students master the foundation facts, they can be used to simplify other unknown facts. When planning mental math themes, it is a good idea to work on building some of these strategies by using the facts associated with them in your themes.

These strategies can be introduced during instruction, but should not be forced during mental math. During mental math, students should share the strategy that works for them. Several strategies should be described during this process. As students become flexible with their computation, their fluency with facts increases.

Addition and Subtraction	
Foundation Facts	
One More	One more is like counting on.
One Less	One less is like counting back.
Two More	Two more is like counting on to the next even or odd number.
Two Less	Two less is like counting back to the previous even or odd number.
Plus Zero	If zero is added, the number remains unchanged or the same. This is easier to memorize; harder to put into context.
Minus Zero	If zero is subtracted, the number remains unchanged or the same.
Ten as an Addend	When adding a one-digit number to 10, it becomes the teen number associated with that one-digit number (e.g., 10 plus 5 becomes 15). Knowing these facts fluently will allow students to simplify facts that are near ten (e.g., 9 + 6 is simplified to 10 + 5).
Ten as the Subtrahend	When subtracting 10 from a teen number, the difference is the digit in the ones place (e.g., 16 − 10 = 6).
Doubles	Using manipulatives and contextual stories can develop doubles facts. In mental math, doubles can be part of a theme: "Double 4, add 2, subtract 1." Fluency with doubles will allow students to use strategies associated with doubles for more difficult facts.

Addition and Subtraction *(continued)*	
Foundation Facts *(continued)*	
Minus Doubles	Once students master doubles, they can easily identify the minus doubles facts by thinking addition (e.g., 12 − 6; think 6 + 6 is 12).
Make Ten	These facts can be developed with ten frames first. Using make ten facts in mental math themes will continue to support mastery of these facts. Knowing these facts will allow students to make ten and add the rest for unknown facts close to ten.
Ten as the Minuend	When 10 is the minuend in a subtraction fact, students can think addition to figure out the missing part that makes 10 (e.g., 10 − 3; think 3 + 7 makes 10).
Building on the Foundations	
Doubles Plus One	Think of addition facts that are one apart as doubles plus one. Students double the smaller number and add one (e.g., 6 + 7; think double 6 is 12, plus 1 is 13).
Doubles plus 2	Addition facts that are two apart can be thought of as doubles plus 2 (e.g., 5 + 7; think double 5 is 10, plus 2 is 12).
Two Apart	Doubling the number between the addends can solve addition facts that are two apart (e.g., 5 + 7; 6 is between 5 and 7, double 6 and get 12).
Make 10 and Extend	Decompose numbers to make ten and add the rest (e.g., 8 + 5, think 8 + 2 + 3; or 8 + 5, think 5 + 5 + 3).
Think Addition for Subtraction	Thinking of the missing addend in an addition problem to solve subtraction—this is the easiest way to do subtraction.
Invented Strategies	Students can invent strategies using patterns and related facts that work for them.

Multiplication and Division	
Foundation Facts	
×2	Students have extensive experience skip counting by twos and grouping twos (pairs) and have developed an understanding of doubling. This set of facts is a natural place to begin exploring multiplication facts (e.g., 6 × 2; think 6 + 6).
×10	The understanding of 10 is foundational in our number system. Students have experienced skip counting by 10, grouping in tens, and working with models of 10, such as ten frames and base-ten blocks (e.g., 5 × 10; think 5 groups of ten, or skip counting by 10s 5 times).
×5	Students have extensive experience skip-counting by 5. They recognize connections with money concepts (nickels). Previous exploration with ×10 facts leads to the insight that multiplying by 5 can be thought of as half of multiplying by 10 (e.g., 5 × 6; think 10 × 6 is 60, half of 60 is 30).
×1	Although ×1 facts are simple to memorize, we do not begin with ×1 facts because of the confusion with the grouping aspect of multiplication (e.g., groups of one?). Providing students with opportunities to explore groups of 2, 5, and 10 provides a stronger foundation for understanding multiplication facts.
×0	×0 facts are easy for students to commit to memory because the product is always 0, but this set of facts can be challenging for the concrete thinkers. It is difficult to conceptualize a group of nothing. Once students have explored multiplication with 2, 10, 5, and 1, this set of facts becomes easier to understand.

Multiplication and Division *(continued)*	
Building on the Foundations	
×3	Multiplying by 3 can be thought of as multiplying by 2 and then adding 1 more group, or as tripling a number.
×4	Multiplying by 4 can be thought of as doubling a double. The previous mastery of ×2 facts allows students to double ×2 products to find the ×4 products.
×6	Multiplying by 6 can be thought of as doubling a multiple of 3. Previous mastery of ×3 facts allows students to see that 4×6 can be thought of as double 4×3, or (4×3) + (4×3). Previous mastery of ×5 facts also supports the students with ×6 facts through knowing that the product of a ×6 fact is simply 1 set more than the product of the related ×5 fact (e.g., the product of 6×8 is 8 more than the product of 5×8).
×9	Building on knowledge of ×10 facts, the product of a ×9 fact is 1 group less than the product of the same ×10 fact (e.g., 10×5=50, so 9×5=45, which is 5 less; or 10×7=70 and 9×7=63, which is 7 less).
×8	Multiplying by 8 results in a product that is double that of multiplying by 4. With the teaching sequence suggested, only two of these facts have not been explored through a different strategy (7×8 and 8×8).
×7	Multiplying by 7 may be the most difficult for students. Students can break apart the 7 (distributive property to find that it is the sum of 5 times the factor and 2 times the factor [e.g., 7×4 is (5×4) + (2×4)]. Although this works, it is more efficient to simply think commutative property and reverse the order of the factors. By doing this students realize that they already know all of the ×7 facts except 7×7.
Think Multiplication for Division	The easiest way to solve division facts is to think multiplication.
Invented Strategies	Students can invent strategies using patterns and related facts that work for them.

Sources: Van De Walle, Karp, and Bay-Williams, 2010; O'Connell and SanGiovanni, 2011a, 2011b.

Philosophy of Teaching Math Facts

This philosophy was developed by Tempe Elementary School District.

In the Tempe Elementary School District, we believe that students learn **basic math facts** by developing **number sense** and the understanding of **number relationships**. Repeated practice with **effective strategies** that develop number sense and understanding of number relationships allows students to **quickly recall basic math facts** and creates **reflective students** who can **think flexibly**.

Math Facts Big Ideas

All math facts are conceptually related; you can learn new or unknown facts from those you already know.

"Think addition" is the most powerful way to learn subtraction.

"Think multiplication" is the most powerful way to learn division.

Multiplication is simply repeated addition, just as division is repeated subtraction.

Three Phases to Mastery of Basic Math Facts

Phase 1: Counting Strategies
Using object counting or verbal counting based on conceptual understanding to determine the answer

Phase 2: Reasoning Strategies
Using known information to logically determine an unknown computation

Phase 3: Mastery
Efficient (fast and accurate) production of the answer

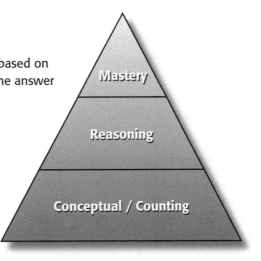

Grade-Level Math Fact Fluency Expectations

Kindergarten: Addition facts with sums to 5 and the related subtraction facts

First Grade: Addition facts with sums to 10 and the related subtraction facts

Second Grade: Addition facts with sums to 20 and the related subtraction facts

Third Grade: Multiplication facts with factors 0–10 within 100 and *related division facts**

Fourth Grade: Division facts related to the third-grade expectations

Fifth Grade: Review and mastery of K–4 expectations

Middle School: Review and mastery of K–4 expectations for students identified through beginning-of-the-year assessment

*This expectation will begin in the 2014/15 school year to align with Common Core standards.

Math Fact Assessment Expectations

90 percent accuracy on the math fact assessments

Addition/Subtraction: 2 minutes for 20 problems

Multiplication/Division: 2 minutes for 25 problems

Frequency of Assessments:
- Beginning of the school year
- Prior to quarterly progress reports
- Prior to quarterly report cards
- End of the school year

Alternate Forms of Assessment

Alternate forms of assessment must follow the above assessment expectations and assessment categories. Alternate forms may include: one-on-one verbal assessments, one-on-one flash cards, podcasts developed by teachers, teacher or adult as scribe for student, teacher-created computer assessments.

Instructional Time Suggestions

Elementary School: replace time spent on math fact drill activities, math intervention time, 5-8 minutes before daily lesson, include in calendar activities, survival box on math review, mental math process.

Middle School: math intervention time, 3–4 minutes before daily lesson, 3–4 minutes after math review quiz, survival box on math review, mental math process, homework practice.

Sources: Ainsworth and Christinson, 2006; O'Connell and SanGiovanni, 2011a, 2011b; Van de Walle and Lovin, 2005a.

Teaching Math Facts Through Math Review and Mental Math

This chart was developed by Tempe Elementary School District.

Operation	Math Review	Mental Math
Addition	**Survival Box:** *How would you add 7 + 8 if you did not know how to do it?* **Explanation:** Students should make their thinking visible by explaining the use of patterns, related facts, and/or any strategies used to find the sum. **Example Response:** *Since 8 is 2 away from 10, I took 2 from 7 and made 10. I then added the remaining 5 from 7 to get 15.* **Modification:** Students who are just learning addition can use pictures to show how to figure out the answer. Encourage the use of ten frames during this learning period. Eventually students should be able to use patterns, related facts, and other mental strategies to find the sums.	Use mental math problems that allow students to compose and decompose numbers and use flexible computation to find multiple ways to approach math facts. **Doubles:** Incorporate <u>doubles</u> in your mental math themes. **Sample Mental Math:** *Double 7, add 4, double your answer.* **Near Doubles:** Incorporate <u>near doubles</u> in your mental math themes after students are proficient with doubles. **Sample Mental Math:** *4 + 5, add 3, double your answer.* **Two Apart Strategy:** Use numbers that are <u>2 apart</u> in your mental math themes after students are proficient with doubles. **Sample Mental Math:** *23 + 25, minus 10, plus 2. (Think 24 + 24 = 48)* **Make Ten Strategy:** Use numbers that allow students to <u>make 10</u> and add the rest. **Sample Mental Math:** *8 + 5, plus 3, minus 5.* **Add 10 and back up:** Add 8 or 9 to bigger numbers in your mental math themes. **Example:** 14 + 8 Think 14 + 10 = 24 and back up 2 to get 22. **Sample Mental Math:** *14 + 8, divided in half, minus 1.*

Operation	Math Review	Mental Math
Subtraction	**Survival Box:** *How would you subtract 17 – 9 if you did not know how to do it?* **Explanation:** Students should make their thinking visible by explaining the use of patterns, related facts, and/or any strategies used to find the answer. **"Think addition" is the most powerful way to become proficient in subtraction.** **Example Responses:** *I thought of addition. I know that when you are subtracting 9 you need to look at the ones digit of the minuend and add one more. So the ones digit of 17 is 7, and one more than 7 is 8.* *9 + 8 = 17, therefore, 17 – 9 = 8.* **Modification:** Students who are just learning subtraction can use pictures to show how to figure out the answer. Encourage them to think of the missing addend as often as possible.	**Think Addition Strategy:** Incorporate the wording that allows students to think addition for subtraction. **Sample Mental Math:** *Five and what number make 13? Add 2 to that number, double your answer.*

Operation	Math Review	Mental Math
Multiplication	**Survival Box:** *How would you multiply 4 × 8 if you did not know how to do it?* **Explanation:** Students should make their thinking visible by explaining the use of patterns, related facts, and/or any strategies used to find the answer. **Example Responses:** *I know my twos. 8 × 2 = 16. I doubled 16 to get 32.* *"I counted by 4s … 4, 8, 12, 16, 20, 24, 28, 32."* **Modification:** Students who are just learning multiplication can use pictures to show how to figure out the answer. Encourage them to draw arrays, sets, etc., to show their understanding of multiplication. Eventually you want them to be able to use patterns, related facts, and other mental strategies to find the products. **Students need to understand that multiplication is repeated addition.**	**Saying Patterns Orally:** Chorally skip count for mental math in order to get students used to the patterns. **Example:** Count by 2s, 5s, 3s, 4s, etc. **Double Numbers:** Frequently <u>double numbers</u> as part of your mental math themes. **Sample Mental Math:** *<u>Double 6</u>, add 3, multiply that by 3.* **Extend:** Include higher products, for example: 8 × 3 doubled gives 8 × 6. **Extend:** Double then double again. **Triple:** Use <u>triples</u> in your mental math themes. **Sample Mental Math:** *2 + 1, <u>triple your answer</u>, add 1.* **Add One More Set:** After saying a multiplication fact students are familiar with, have them <u>add another set</u>. **Sample Mental Math:** *5 × 7, <u>add another set of seven</u>.*

Operation	Math Review	Mental Math
Division	**Survival Box:** *How would you divide 35 ÷ 5 if you did not know how to do it?* **Explanation:** Students should make their thinking visible by explaining the use of patterns, related facts, and/or any strategies used to find the answer. **Example Response:** *I thought about multiplication. I know that 5 × 7 = 35, so 35 ÷ 5 = 7.* **Modification:** Students who are just learning division can use pictures to show how to figure out the answer. Eventually students should be able to determine the answer to division by thinking multiplication. **Students also need to understand that division is simply repeated subtraction.**	**Think Multiplication Strategy:** Incorporate the wording that allows students to <u>think multiplication</u> for division. **Sample Mental Math:** *Five multiplied by what number makes 45? Add 5 to that number, then double it.*

Math Facts Glossary

This glossary was developed by Tempe Elementary School District.

Addend: A number that is involved in addition. Numbers being added are called addends.

Addition and subtraction within 5, 10, 20, 100, or 1000: Addition or subtraction of two whole numbers with whole number answers, and with sum or minuend in the range 0–5, 0–10, 0–20, or 0–100, respectively. Example: $8 + 2 = 10$ is an addition within 10, $14 - 5 = 9$ is a subtraction within 20, and $55 - 18 = 37$ is a subtraction within 100.

Associative property of addition: The addition of a set of numbers is the same regardless of how the numbers are grouped.

Associative property of multiplication: The multiplication of a set of numbers is the same regardless of how the numbers are grouped.

Basic math facts: Addition or multiplication facts where addends or factors are less than 10. This includes the subtraction and division facts related to the addition and multiplication facts.

Commutative property of addition: Changing the order of the addends does not change the sum.

Commutative property of multiplication: Changing the order of the factors does not change the product.

Composing numbers: Putting numbers together.

Counting on: A strategy for finding the number of objects in a group without having to count every member of the group. For example, if a stack of books is known to have 8 books and 3 more books are added to the top, it is not necessary to count the stack all over again. One can find the total by counting on—pointing to the top book and saying "eight," then following this with "nine, ten, eleven. There are eleven books now."

Decomposing numbers: Breaking numbers apart.

Difference: The amount that remains after one quantity is subtracted from another.

Dividend: The total amount that you want to divide.

Divisor: The number by which you divide.

Factor: A number that is involved in multiplication. The numbers you multiply together are called factors.

Flexible computation: Involves taking apart and combining numbers in a variety of ways. Most partitions of numbers are based on place value or "compatible" numbers—number pairs that work easily together.

Identity property of addition: The identity property of addition states that the sum of zero and any number or variable is the number or variable itself.

Identity property of multiplication: The identity property of multiplication states that the product of 1 and any number or variable is the number or variable itself.

Minuend: A number from which the subtrahend is to be subtracted.

Multiplication and division within 100: Multiplication or division of two whole numbers with whole number answers, and with the product or dividend in the range 0–100. Example: $72 \div 8 = 9$.

Number sense: Understanding the relationship between and among numbers; having the ability to think flexibly about numbers and to break numbers apart and put them back together; being familiar with the properties of single-digit numbers and using this information to calculate efficiently using larger numbers; having the ability to manipulate numbers in your head; having effective ways to estimate.

Product: The answer when two or more numbers are multiplied together.

Subtrahend: The number that is being subtracted.

Sum: The answer when two or more numbers are added together.

Quotient: The answer after you divide one number by another.

Math Facts Instructional Strategies for Teaching Addition and Subtraction

These strategies are from Tempe Elementary School District.

Instructional Strategy	Description	Examples
Number Sense: Making sets	Students need experience with making sets of objects. This will allow them to get a sense of quantity. Repeated practice of this strategy is essential to building number sense. As students become more comfortable with making sets, they will be able to change the quantity without recounting. Example: They have 2 on their math mat, and you ask them to show 4. A student with good number sense will not need to recount. They will be able to add 2 more.	**Grouping**: Whole group or small group **Manipulatives:** Counters, chips, pennies, cubes, paper clips, etc. **Math Mat:** Can be a whiteboard, laminated construction paper, tray, ten frame, etc. **Procedure**: Model making sets of numbers 0–5 on your math mat with the manipulative of your choice. Students will practice making sets on their math mat. "Show me what 2 looks like." "Show me what 0 looks like." Continue with various numbers 0–5. Be sure to have some discussions about how students made their sets. **Extension:** When students have good number sense with 0–5, continue to 10, 15, 20.
Number Sense: Counting sets	Students need experience counting sets of objects in order to build number sense. As students become more comfortable counting sets, they will have an automaticity of matching the visual with the quantity.	**Grouping**: Whole group or small group **Materials:** Dot cards, dot plates, dice, counters, cubes, ten frames, math books, etc. **Procedure**: Choose one of the listed materials, and model how you count the set. Continue showing various sets (0–5) with the same materials you have chosen, and have the students count the set. In a small-group setting students should have the set in front of them and use one-to-one correspondence if needed to count the set. Be sure to check for understanding after each set. Ask students to explain how they know the answer. **Extension:** When students have good number sense with 0–5, continue to 10, 15, 20.

Instructional Strategy	Description	Examples
Number Sense: Number stories for addition and subtraction	It is important for students to build number sense through number stories. This should be done without attaching the numbers, symbols, and operations at first. Tell number stories to your students and have them use manipulatives, act it out, draw it. Be sure to make the stories fun and interesting in order to hold their attention. This can be done by using names of students in your classroom and incorporating things they are interested in.	**Grouping**: Whole group or small group **Manipulatives:** Counters, chips, pennies, cubes, paper clips, paper, crayons, etc. **Procedure**: Tell a number story and model your thinking as you figure out the answer. Lisa's dog ate two treats. She gave him one more. How many does he eat now? I know the dog ate two, then one more. I think my answer will be more than two. If I put two blocks to represent the treats and add one more that makes 3. Continue with number stories having students work to find the answer. Students should partner-share their answer and reasoning. **Extension**: As students become proficient with this, challenge them to do the math in their head for sums and differences 0–5.
Number Sense: Up and back counting	Fluency in counting will be essential in building number sense. Students need frequent short practice with counting skills.	**Grouping**: Whole group **Procedure**: Have five students stand in front of a row of chairs. As the class counts each student, the child counted sits down. When you reach the target number (5), it is repeated. The child who sat on five, stands up again and is counted as 5. The child before him stands and is counted as 4, etc. 1, 2, 3, 4, 5, 5, 4, 3, 2, 1. Do this with different target numbers.
Number Sense: Counting on with counters	Students need frequent experience starting with numbers other than one when counting.	**Grouping**: Whole Group **Procedure**: Hide a number of counters in your hand. Place more counters in a line next to your hand. Have students practice counting up by saying the number of counters in your hand and then counting the extra counters. **Example:** 　　　　3　　　4　　　5 Do this with different target numbers.

Instructional Strategy	Description	Examples
Number Sense: Spatial relationships	Seeing the patterns of numbers spatially allows students to build instant recognition of numbers.	**Grouping:** Whole group or small group **Manipulatives:** Dominoes, dot cards, dot plates, dice, counters, cubes, ten frames, math books, etc. **Procedure:** Hold up a dot card for 2–5 seconds. Ask students how many dots they saw. Students should respond with the number of dots and justification for their answer. In order to build confidence, start with lots of easy and familiar patterns of numbers (like the ones seen on dice). **Extension:** Hold up a domino for 1–5 seconds. Ask students to mentally add both sides of the domino. They should say the sum and justify their answer.
Number Sense: One and two more, one and two less	Students need to be able to manipulate numbers and see their relationship to other numbers. **Example:** 7 is 1 more than 6 and 2 less than 9	**Grouping:** Whole group or small group **Manipulatives:** Dominos, dot cards, numeral cards **Procedure:** Use dominoes and play the usual way, but instead of matching the ends, a new domino can be added if it has an end that is one less than the end on the board. This can also be done with one more, two less, and two more. **Alternate Procedure:** Give students about six different dot cards. The students will then need to construct a set of counters that is two more than the set shown on the card. **Alternate Procedure:** Similarly, spread out eight to ten dot cards and the students will need to find another card for each that is two less than the card shown. **Extension:** Teacher can mix in dot cards and numeral cards. Students can also be encouraged to take turns reading the number sentence to their partner. Example: "Two more than four is six."

Instructional Strategy	Description	Examples
Number Sense: Anchoring numbers to 5 and 10	Students need to relate a given number to other numbers. This relationship is key when students are developing number combinations.	**Grouping:** Whole group or small group **Manipulatives:** Five frame, ten frame *It is important to use the five frame if students have not yet been exposed to the ten frame. **Procedure:** All children have their own ten frames (or five frames). The teacher will call out a random number. After each number, the students will need to change their frame to show the new number. Look for students who are wiping off their whole frame, compared to those who know to just add or subtract a few. Encourage discussion about adding or removing to change the frame rather than wiping it clean. **Extension:** Use ten frame flash cards. Flash the cards and have students identify the number chorally. **Variations:** • Have students say the number of empty spaces on the card instead of the number of dots. • Have students say a number that is one more (two more, one less, two less) than the number of dots. • Have the students say the "ten fact" based on the number of dots on the ten frame. **Example:** "Six and four make ten."

Instructional Strategy	Description	Examples
Number Sense: Part-part-whole relationships	Students need to understand that there are different number combinations (parts) that make up a number (whole). This is called a part-part-whole relationship. This is a great strategy for the make ten facts.	**Grouping:** Whole group or small group **Manipulatives:** Mat, two-sided counters, unifix cubes, dot strips, two-column strips, etc. **Procedure:** Students should have one set of manipulatives (cubes, counters, etc.). Their job is to see how many different combinations for a certain number they can make using two parts. Students should display each different combination on their mat. Ask students to then read their number sentence that goes with their combination. **Extension:** This is called 2 out of 3. Make a list of three numbers, two of which total the whole that the students are focusing on. Examples for 5: 2 – 3 – 4 5 – 0 – 2 1 – 3 – 2 3 – 1 – 4 2 – 2 – 3 4 – 3 – 1 The students should choose the two numbers that make the whole and justify their answer.
Number Sense: Missing parts	The missing part can be found with the relationship between the other part and the whole.	**Grouping:** Whole group or small group **Manipulatives:** Counters, cup, missing part cards **Procedure:** First count out the amount you are focusing on so the students know the whole. Next, cover up any part of that whole. Prompt the students to automatically say the number sentence. **Example:** If 5 is the whole and only 2 are showing, the student should say "2 and 3 is 5." **Extension:** I wish I had: Show (with any manipulative) dots showing less than a target number. Say, "I wish I had (the target number)." Students should respond with the amount needed to make the target number. "You need (missing part) more." **Example:** Teacher: "I have **4**, I wish I had **6**." Students: "You need **2** more."

Instructional Strategy	Description	Examples
Number Sense: Doubles	Students need to develop fluency with doubles facts. This will build a foundation for using doubles facts as anchors for other number combinations such as doubles plus 1 or doubles plus 2.	**Grouping:** Whole group or small group **Manipulatives:** Picture cards (for each double) that can be used to create word problems **Procedure:** Show students the picture cards. Students use the picture card to create a word problem. Alex and Zack each found 7 seashells at the beach. How many did they find together?

Using Related Facts:
 	
Doubles plus one
	After students have a good foundation of doubles.
	
	Includes all combinations where one addend is one more than the other.
	
	The strategy is to double the smaller number and add one.
	
	Students need to be able to match the near double with the double.
		Near Double Double
		    4 + 3 3 + 3
		Use linking cubes to show near doubles.
		
		This will illustrate the concept of doubles plus one.
		Make the doubles fact one color and the plus one portion a different color.
		Show students a list of near doubles and have them circle the smaller number. They should double the smaller number and write it under the number.
		Finally, they would add one to get the answer
		
		    5 + ④ = 9
		          8
		
		As students become proficient, move them into the abstract by having them visualize this in their heads.

Number Sense: Doubles plus one	Doubles plus one will allow students to build upon the anchor of doubles when faced with other number combinations.	**Grouping:** Whole group or small group **Manipulatives:** Equation cards with doubles, equation cards with doubles plus one **Procedure:** Have students spread out the doubles equation cards. Once all cards are down, have students pick up the doubles plus one equation cards and place each equation card over the doubles fact that helps.

Instructional Strategy	Description	Examples
Using Related Facts: Doubles plus two	Similar to doubles plus one; use after students have a foundation of doubles and doubles plus one. Includes combinations where one addend is two more than the other. Students need to be able to match the near doubles with the doubles.	Near Double: 5 + 3 Double: 3 + 3 Use linking cubes to show near doubles. This will illustrate the concept of doubles plus two. Make the doubles fact one color and the plus two portion a different color. Show students a list of near doubles and have them circle the smaller number. They should double it and write it underneath. Finally, they would add two to write the answer 6 + ④ = 10 8 As students become proficient, move them into the abstract by having them visualize this in their head.
Using Related Facts: Two apart facts	Similar to doubles plus two; use after students have a foundation of doubles and doubles plus one. Students need to be able to decompose numbers. Includes combinations where one addend is two more than the other. You double the number between the two addends.	Near Double: 5 + 3 Double: 3 + 3 New Double: 4 + 4 = 8 As students become proficient, move them into the abstract by having them visualize this in their head.

Instructional Strategy	Description	Examples
Number Sense: Anchor of ten, making 10	Students can use the anchor of ten to help solve equations that have larger numbers.	**Grouping:** Whole group or small group **Manipulatives:** Ten frames, equation cards (flash cards) **Procedure:** Give students two ten frames. Place the flash cards face down next to the ten frames (or you can orally give the fact). Students need to first model each number on the two ten frames and then decide on the easiest way to show the number (do not allow counting). The goal is to have students move some of the counters to make a whole ten frame and put the remainder on the other ten frame. Focus on making that ten. Example: $$\begin{array}{r} 9 \\ +\,8 \\ \hline \end{array}$$ Students could move one from 8 to make ten or could move 2 from 9 to make ten. When first doing this activity, focus only on equations with 9s and 8s until students understand the concept of trading a couple to make ten. **Extension:** You can use the same concept with subtraction flash cards, making sure once again to start with equations using 8 and 9. Have students make ten in a frame first.
Using Related Facts: Make ten	Students need to know how to combine any single-digit number with 10 (10 + 5 = 15). Works well with addends of 8 and 9. Students need to know how to compose and decompose numbers. Take what is needed from the smaller number to make the larger number 10, and add the leftovers to find the sum.	Below is an example of how to visually show the students what you are doing. $$\begin{array}{r} 7 \\ +\,9 \\ \hline \end{array}$$ Move 1 to make 10. 7 plus 9 is the same as 10 and 6: 16. As students become proficient, move them into the abstract by having them visualize this in their head.

Instructional Strategy	Description	Examples
Using Related Facts: Make ten and extend	Students need to know how to combine any single-digit number with 10 (10 + 5 = 15). Works well with 7 and 5 as addends. Students need to know how to compose and decompose numbers. Take the amount you need to make 10 and add the leftovers.	Similar to photo in previous section, but with 7 or 5. For example: 7 + 5 could be done by taking 3 from the 5 to make 10 and adding the leftover 2 to equal 12. 7 + 5 could also be done by taking 5 from the 7 to combine with the other 5 to make 10 and adding the leftover 2 to make 12.
Using Related Facts: The generic task	Students are posed with a fact. They then discuss with a partner a strategy used to solve the fact. The strategy is shared with the class. Encourage students to find multiple ways to solve the fact. Use the think–pair–share approach. This method gives every student the message that his or her idea is okay.	If you do not know the answer to 8 + 5, what are some efficient ways to get to the answer? Efficient means you don't have to count, and you do it in your head. **Possible answer:** Making ten by adding 8 + 2, then adding the remaining 3
Using Number Sense: Reason- ableness	Students should be taught and expected to think about the reasonableness of their answers. They should be asked to defend the reasonableness of their answers on several occasions.	Does this answer make sense? Is this answer reasonable? Is the sum greater than the two addends?
Commutative Property	The order of the addends does not change the sum.	7 + 8 = 15 8 + 7 = 15 Teach students that by understanding the commutative property they only have to master 55 of the 100 addition facts.
Using Related Facts for Subtraction	"Think addition" is the most efficient way to teach subtraction. Teach students to think of the missing part or addend in the related addition fact.	14 − 9 = ____ Think 9 + what number = 14? The answer is 5.

Source: Van de Walle and Lovin, 2005a; Van de Walle, Karp, and Bay-Williams, 2010.

Math Facts Instructional Strategies for Teaching Multiplication and Division

These strategies are from Tempe Elementary School District.

Instructional Strategy	Description	Examples
Using Models and Related Facts: Equal groups	Students need several opportunities to work with models when learning the concept of multiplication. Use counters, chips, cubes, base-10 blocks, and other concrete materials to show multiplication, repeated addition, or sets of numbers.	Show students that addition is related to multiplication. 3 groups of 4 is like adding. $4 + 4 + 4 = 12$ We can also multiply. $3 \times 4 = 12$
Using Models: Area models or arrays	Building area models or arrays is a connection to geometry. By showing multiplication as an array, we teach students why we use multiplication to find the area of rectangles. It is important to make this connection.	Help students build construction paper arrays on the carpet to model multiplication with 2s and 5s. Use grid paper and have students create arrays and write the corresponding multiplication fact. **Extension**: Give students a product and challenge them to create all of the arrays that have that area.
Using Models and Patterns: Number line	Using the number line models skip-counting patterns for students. Allow students to have multiple opportunities experimenting with skip counting on the number line to find the product in multiplication problems.	 This example shows $4 \times 5 = 20$ Students can also practice skip counting on the number line or hundreds chart by circling the multiples and counting. 5, 10, 15, 20, 25, 30 …

Instructional Strategy	Description	Examples
Using Patterns: All facts	As students become proficient in skip-counting patterns, have them examine the patterns more closely. Encourage students to find the pattern in the ones place to predict higher multiples. Extension Questions: Could you have a multiple of 6 with a 5 in the ones place?	**Twos:** The digit in the ones place repeats: 2, 4, 6, 8, 0, 2, 4, 6, 8, 0 … **Threes**: The digit in the ones place repeats: 3, 6, 9, 2, 5, 8, 1, 4, 7, 0, 3, 6, 9, 2, 5, 8, 1, 4, 7, 0 … The sum of the digits adds to 3 or a multiple of three: $7 \times 3 = 21 \ 2 + 1 = 3$ $8 \times 3 = 24 \ 2 + 4 = 6$ $55 \times 3 = 165 \ 1 + 6 + 5 = 12; \ 1 + 2 = 3$ **Fours:** The digit in the ones place repeats: 4, 8, 2, 6, 0, 4, 8, 2, 6, 0 … **Fives:** The digit in the ones place repeats: 5, 0, 5, 0 … **Sixes:** The digit in the ones place repeats: 6, 2, 8, 4, 0, 6, 2, 8, 4, 0 … **Sevens:** This is one of the more difficult patterns. The digit in the ones place repeats: 7, 4, 1, 8, 5, 2, 9, 6, 3, 0, 7, 4, 1, 8, 5, 2, 9, 6, 3, 0, 7… **Eights:** The digit in the ones place repeats: 8, 6, 4, 2, 0, 8, 6, 4, 2, 0 … **Nines:** The digit in the ones place repeats, and also decreases by one: 9, 8, 7, 6, 5, 4, 3, 2, 1, 0, 9, 8, 7, 6, 5, 4, 3, 2, 1, 0… The sum of the digits is always 9: $3 \times 9 = 27 \ 2 + 7 = 9$ $15 \times 9 = 135 \ 1 + 3 + 5 = 9$ **Tens:** The digit in the ones place is always 0.
Using Related Facts: Twos	The doubles addition facts are related to multiplication facts with a factor of two. Students who have addition mastered should quickly master their twos. Help students make this connection by making flash cards with the related doubles addition fact.	When multiplying by two you need to double the other factor by adding it twice. $2 \times ⑦ = 7 + 7 = 14$
Using Patterns: Fives and tens	Help students connect counting by 5s and 10s with multiplication.	Practice counting groups of fives and groups of ten. Help students see the patterns in the ones digit for each. 4 x 5 (think 5, 10, 15, 20) 3 x 10 (think 10, 20, 30) Relate the fives facts to the clock and how counting by fives helps tell time in 5-minute increments.

Instructional Strategy	Description	Examples
Using Number Sense: Zero property, identity property	There are 36 facts that have either 0 or 1 as a factor. Students sometimes get the rules of these facts confused with the rules of addition. $6 + 0 = 6$ (stays the same) $6 \times 0 = 0$ (always 0) $6 + 1 = 7$ (one more) $6 \times 1 = 6$ (stays the same) It is best to develop the concept instead of the rule by using story problems and real-life situations. Avoid rules such as "any number multiplied by zero is zero."	Johnny is trying to catch bugs for a school project. He has six jars. He has nothing in each jar. How many bugs does he have? $6 \times 0 = 0$ Lucia is planting flowers. She has 4 pots. She planted one flower in each pot. How many flowers does she have? $4 \times 1 = 4$ Lucia is planting flowers. She has one pot. She planted 4 flowers in the pot. How many flowers does she have? $1 \times 4 = 4$
Using Patterns and Related Facts: Nines	Many students love learning the nines because there are several patterns that are fun to discover. Help students discover the patterns on their own. These are patterns in the multiplication system, not "rules."	Write a list of all of the nine facts and have students work together to discover as many patterns as possible. After discovering and discussing the patterns, have students come up with a clever strategy to figure out a nine fact if they don't know it. **Possible Strategies:** • The tens digit is always one less than the other factor, and when added to the ones digit, the sum is nine. 7×9 (think one less than 7 is 6. 6 plus 3 is 9) The answer is 63 • The product is always one set less than the product of the factor times 10. 7×9 (think 7×10 is 70. $70 - 7$ is 63) The answer is 63

Instructional Strategy	Description	Examples
Using Related Facts: Helping facts	Once students have mastered the 2s, 5s, 10s 0s, 1s, and 9s, there are only 25 facts left to master.	Give students a blank multiplication chart and have them follow along as you fill in the products of the twos, fives, tens, zeros, ones, and nines. Have the students use a highlighter to color the 25 empty boxes that are remaining. Tell students that you are going to help them create and learn several strategies for mastering the remaining 25 facts.
	It is encouraging to students do discover this by filling in a multiplication chart.	<table><tr><td>X</td><td>0</td><td>1</td><td>2</td><td>3</td><td>4</td><td>5</td><td>6</td><td>7</td><td>8</td><td>9</td></tr><tr><td>0</td><td>0</td><td>0</td><td>0</td><td>0</td><td>0</td><td>0</td><td>0</td><td>0</td><td>0</td><td>0</td></tr><tr><td>1</td><td>0</td><td>1</td><td>2</td><td>3</td><td>4</td><td>5</td><td>6</td><td>7</td><td>8</td><td>9</td></tr><tr><td>2</td><td>0</td><td>2</td><td>4</td><td>6</td><td>8</td><td>10</td><td>12</td><td>13</td><td>16</td><td>18</td></tr><tr><td>3</td><td>0</td><td>3</td><td>6</td><td></td><td></td><td>15</td><td></td><td></td><td></td><td>27</td></tr><tr><td>4</td><td>0</td><td>4</td><td>8</td><td></td><td></td><td>20</td><td></td><td></td><td></td><td>36</td></tr><tr><td>5</td><td>0</td><td>5</td><td>10</td><td>15</td><td>20</td><td>25</td><td>30</td><td>35</td><td>40</td><td>45</td></tr><tr><td>6</td><td>0</td><td>6</td><td>12</td><td></td><td></td><td>30</td><td></td><td></td><td></td><td>54</td></tr><tr><td>7</td><td>0</td><td>7</td><td>14</td><td></td><td></td><td>35</td><td></td><td></td><td></td><td>63</td></tr><tr><td>8</td><td>0</td><td>8</td><td>16</td><td></td><td></td><td>40</td><td></td><td></td><td></td><td>72</td></tr><tr><td>9</td><td>0</td><td>9</td><td>18</td><td>27</td><td>36</td><td>45</td><td>54</td><td>63</td><td>72</td><td>81</td></tr></table>
Double and add a Set (threes)	For facts with a factor of 3, double the other factor then add another set.	3 × 7 (think 2 × 7 is 14, another 7 is 21) **or** (think double 7 is 14, add another set of 7 and get 21)
Double and double again (fours)	When facts have a 4 as one of the factors, students can double the other factor then double it again. It is like using the related two fact.	4 × 7 (think double 7 is 14, double 14 is 28) **or** (think 2 × 7 is 14, double 14 and get 28)
Double, double, double (eights)	Applying the "double, double, double" strategy can solve facts with 8 as a factor. Doubling the other factor 3 times in a row results in the product.	8 × 6 (think double 6 is 12, double 12 is 24, double 24 is 48)
Half then double (sixes and eights)	If either factor is even, students can use the "half then double" strategy. Select the even factor and cut it in half. Find the product of this new problem and double the answer. This works well with sixes and eights.	6 × 8 (think half of 6 is 3, 3 × 8 is 24, double 24 and get 48) **or** (think half of 8 is 4, 6 × 4 is 24, double 24 and get 48)
Add one more set (any fact)	Students can use a helping fact that they know and add one more set to find the product of a fact they don't know.	6 × 7 (think 5 × 7 is 35 and one more 7 is 42) **or** (think 6 × 6 is 36 and one more 6 is 42)

Instructional Strategy	Description	Examples
Properties of Multiplication	Students need to understand the properties of multiplication in order to be successful with their facts. It allows them to be flexible in their computation in a variety of ways.	 $2 \times 3 \quad = \quad 3 \times 2$ $6 \quad = \quad 6$
Commutative property of multiplication	Develop the understanding that you can multiply the two factors in any order and get the same product.	Students should draw and build arrays to gain understanding of why this property is true.
Distributive property of multiplication	It is very useful to understand how the distributive property works. It is another great strategy to use in order to find the product of an unknown fact.	$5 \times 7 = 5 \times (5 + 2) = (5 \times 5) + (5 \times 2)$ $\mathbf{5 \times 7 = 35}$ $\mathbf{5 \times 5 = 25} \quad 2 \times 5 = 10 \quad \mathbf{25 + 10 = 35}$

Instructional Strategy	Description	Examples
Using Related Facts for Division	Develop the understanding of the relationship between multiplication and division.	 FACTOR FACTOR PRODUCT DIVIDEND DIVISOR QUOTIENT $3 \times 6 = 18$ $18 \div 3 = 6$ number of groups number in each group number in all number of groups number in each group number in all Show students how the parts of a multiplication problem relate to the parts of a division problem (i.e., fact families) Example: $4 \times 5 = 20$ $5 \times 4 = 20$ $20 \div 5 = 4$ $20 \div 4 = 5$
	The most powerful way for students to master division facts is by using the "think multiplication" strategy.	$45 \div 9$ (think, "What number multiplied by 9 is 45?" The answer is 5)

Instructional Strategy	Description	Examples
Additional Activities	How long? How many?	**Materials:** Cuisenaire rods, dice, centimeter grid paper
		Activity: Each student will use a different 10 × 10 centimeter grid paper. One student will roll the dice twice. The first roll tells how long of a rod to use and the second roll will tell how many rods to use. Then a student will arrange the rods into a rectangle and trace it onto their grid paper. Then the student will write the corresponding multiplication in each rectangle. Continue until there is no room left to draw any more rectangles.
	The factor game	**Materials:** Markers in two different colors, a sheet of paper with the numbers 1–30
		Activity: Each student uses different color markers. One student selects a number and circles it with his or her marker. The other student finds all the proper factors of that number, circling each with his or her marker in a different color. The process alternates between the two students until there are no factors left for the remaining numbers. Students add the numbers they circled. The winner is the student with the larger score.
	Commutative property of multiplication for use with 5s	Provide student pairs with 10 counters. Have the students put the counters in two vertical rows of 5 counters each. Explain that the columns represent two groups.
		Ask: "How many are in each group?" "What multiplication problem would this be?"
		After discussion have students put the counters into two horizontal rows of five counters each.
		Ask: "How many vertical groups can you make?"
		"What multiplication problem would this be?"
		Discuss the commutative property of multiplication and how this demonstrates it.
		Distribute 5 more counters and repeat with vertical and horizontal groups of five.
	Relate addition and multiplication, for use with 2s (can be modified to illustrate how multiplication and division are related)	Provide student pairs with 8 counters. Have the students place the counters into 2 equal groups.
		Ask: "What addition problem could this be?"
		Have the students mix up the counters again into a group of 8. Once again, group into 2 groups of 4. Explain that in multiplication the first number is the number of groups and the second number is the number in each group, so 4 + 4 is the same as 2 × 4.
		Distribute 2 more counters and model 5 + 5 and 2 × 5. Have students illustrate two vertical rows of 6 and ask them to create an addition and a multiplication problem for the 12 chips.
		*This activity can be reviewed in Math Review by drawing arrays representing 14, 18, and 20. Have the students show and explain the addition and multiplication problems for the arrays.

Instructional Strategy	Description	Examples
Additional Activities *(continued)*	My finger is sore	Present students with an imaginary scenario that you had to go to Subway and buy 8 sandwiches that cost $4 dollars each. Show that you had to push the 4 key on the calculator 8 times to find the total cost.
		Ask: "Is there another way to find the cost more quickly?"
		"What else could I have done besides 4 + 4 + 4 + 4 + 4 + 4 + 4 + 4?"
		Discussion: You can skip count or multiply.
		Ask: "What would happen if you grouped the two 4s together to form 8?"
		"What would that problem now be?"
		"If you grouped two 8s together, what would the problem be?"
		"What if you put the 8s together?"
		4 + 4 + 4 + 4 + 4 + 4 + 4 + 4 (8×4)
		8 + 8 + 8 + 8 (4×8)
		16 + 16 (2×16)
		*This can be reviewed in Math Review with other examples, such as 4×9, 6×3, and 8×5.

Sources: Van de Walle and Lovin, 2005a; Maletsky, et al., 2004.

Math Facts Record Keeping

This chart is from Tempe Elementary School District.

Second Grade	First Grade Review	+ 10	– 10	Add Doubles	Subtract Doubles	Make 10s (8–9)	Subtract from 10	Doubles Plus 1	Doubles Plus 2	Make 10 and Extend	Addition/Subtraction Final			
20														
19														
18														
17														
16														
15														
14														
13														
12														
11														
10														
9														
8														
7														
6														
5														
4														
3														
2														
1														
Score														
Date														

Achievement goal for each quiz is 90 percent correct or better.

Math Facts Assessments

These assessments are from Tempe Elementary School District.

Grade 2

Grade 2   Name _____

(First Grade Addition Review)   Score _____ / 20

You have 2 minutes to complete this assessment.

4	5	7	6	4
+ 6	+ 5	+ 1	+ 1	+ 2

4	5	7	6	4
+ 6	+ 5	+ 1	+ 1	+ 2

4	5	7	6	4
+ 6	+ 5	+ 1	+ 1	+ 2

4	5	7	6	4
+ 6	+ 5	+ 1	+ 1	+ 2

Grade 2   Name _____

(First Grade Subtraction Review)   Score _____ / 20

You have 2 minutes to complete this assessment.

8	6	7	9	4
− 2	− 3	− 5	− 3	− 0

6	7	6	3	8
− 4	− 2	− 1	− 0	− 4

10	9	5	9	10
− 3	− 7	− 5	− 8	− 5

7	3	8	5	9
− 5	− 1	− 6	− 4	− 5

Grade 2   Name _____

(Add 10)   Score _____ / 20

You have 2 minutes to complete this assessment.

10 + 2	5 + 10	10 + 4	10 + 3	10 + 5
6 + 10	10 + 8	3 + 10	10 + 3	9 + 10
10 + 5	2 + 10	10 + 4	10 + 6	10 + 1
7 + 10	10 + 9	1 + 10	10 + 0	8 + 10

Grade 2   Name _____

(Add 10, Review)   Score _____ / 20

You have 2 minutes to complete this assessment.

10 + 4	0 + 8	8 + 10	2 + 7	10 + 3
6 + 10	9 + 1	10 + 1	8 + 1	10 + 9
2 + 10	5 + 2	6 + 10	1 + 6	0 + 10
10 + 7	0 + 6	10 + 5	9 + 2	1 + 10

Grade 2   Name _____

(Subtract 10)   Score _____ / 20

You have 2 minutes to complete this assessment.

20 − 10	18 − 10	16 − 10	10 − 10	14 − 10
11 − 10	16 − 10	19 − 10	13 − 10	12 − 10
15 − 10	11 − 10	13 − 10	17 − 10	16 − 10
18 − 10	10 − 10	14 − 10	12 − 10	15 − 10

Grade 2   Name _____

(Subtract 10, Review)   Score _____ / 20

You have 2 minutes to complete this assessment.

18 − 10	18 − 2	16 − 10	14 − 2	19 − 10
12 − 10	10 − 1	15 − 10	17 − 0	14 − 10
13 − 10	16 − 2	17 − 10	13 − 1	20 − 10
11 − 10	9 − 1	10 − 10	15 − 0	18 − 10

Grade 2   Name _____

(Add Doubles)   Score _____ / 20

You have 2 minutes to complete this assessment.

2 + 2	5 + 5	6 + 6	3 + 3	4 + 4
5 + 5	1 + 1	7 + 7	4 + 4	9 + 9
6 + 6	8 + 8	1 + 1	2 + 2	7 + 7
3 + 3	4 + 4	2 + 2	8 + 8	7 + 7

Grade 2   Name _____

(Add Doubles, Review)   Score _____ / 20

You have 2 minutes to complete this assessment.

2 + 2	2 + 6	7 + 7	2 + 6	4 + 3
5 + 5	9 + 2	3 + 3	4 + 2	9 + 9
4 + 4	3 + 2	6 + 6	2 + 9	5 + 5
2 + 5	5 + 6	8 + 8	5 + 2	9 + 1

Grade 2   Name _____

(Subtract Doubles)   Score _____ / 20

You have 2 minutes to complete this assessment.

4 − 2	10 − 5	2 − 1	6 − 3	8 − 4
12 − 6	18 − 9	6 − 3	8 − 4	14 − 7
10 − 5	16 − 8	12 − 6	20 − 10	10 − 5
18 − 9	14 − 7	4 − 2	16 − 8	2 − 1

Grade 2   Name _____

(Subtract Doubles, Review)   Score _____ / 20

You have 2 minutes to complete this assessment.

4 − 2	10 − 5	12 − 10	6 − 2	8 − 4
18 − 10	12 − 6	6 − 3	7 − 2	14 − 7
18 − 9	15 − 10	13 − 10	5 − 2	20 − 2
16 − 8	8 − 2	14 − 10	11 − 2	9 − 0

Grade 2   Name _____

(Make 10)   Score _____ / 20

You have 2 minutes to complete this assessment.

8 + 2	9 + 1	2 + 8	3 + 7	4 + 6
5 + 5	10 + 0	3 + 7	0 + 10	1 + 9
6 + 4	3 + 7	2 + 8	7 + 3	5 + 5
1 + 9	3 + 7	9 + 1	10 + 0	7 + 3

Grade 2   Name _____

(Make 10, Review)   Score _____ / 20

You have 2 minutes to complete this assessment.

10 + 4	5 + 5	3 + 7	2 + 9	4 + 6
6 + 6	9 + 1	1 + 10	8 + 8	7 + 3
2 + 9	5 + 10	7 + 7	0 + 6	2 + 5
7 + 3	4 + 6	6 + 2	4 + 4	7 + 2

Grade 2 Name _____

(Subtract from 10) Score _____ / 20

You have 2 minutes to complete this assessment.

10	10	10	10	10
− 1	− 0	− 5	− 8	− 2

10	10	10	10	10
− 3	− 6	− 4	− 7	− 1

10	10	10	10	10
− 9	− 10	− 3	− 5	− 8

10	10	10	10	10
− 0	− 4	− 2	− 9	− 6

Grade 2 Name _____

(Subtract from 10, Review) Score _____ / 20

You have 2 minutes to complete this assessment.

10	8	4	10	11
− 4	− 1	− 4	− 5	− 2

15	14	10	18	4
− 10	− 7	− 6	− 9	− 2

10	16	12	5	10
− 3	− 8	− 6	− 2	− 8

7	9	10	7	10
− 2	− 2	− 9	− 1	− 2

Grade 2   Name _____

(Doubles Plus 1)   Score _____ / 20

You have 2 minutes to complete this assessment.

2 + 3	5 + 6	7 + 6	4 + 3	4 + 5
6 + 5	1 + 2	7 + 8	5 + 4	9 + 8
6 + 7	8 + 9	2 + 1	3 + 2	8 + 7
3 + 3	8 + 7	9 + 8	6 + 7	3 + 4

Grade 2   Name _____

(Doubles Plus 1, Review)   Score _____ / 20

You have 2 minutes to complete this assessment.

2 + 2	6 + 5	7 + 8	2 + 6	5 + 4
5 + 5	9 + 2	3 + 4	8 + 8	10 + 9
4 + 2	3 + 2	7 + 6	2 + 9	5 + 6
9 + 8	0 + 6	8 + 2	5 + 4	9 + 1

Grade 2　　　　　　　　　Name _____

(Doubles Plus 2)　　　　　　　　　　　　　　　Score _____ / 20

You have 2 minutes to complete this assessment.

2 + 4	5 + 7	7 + 9	4 + 6	3 + 5
6 + 8	1 + 3	7 + 5	6 + 4	9 + 7
5 + 7	8 + 6	4 + 6	3 + 5	5 + 7
7 + 9	6 + 4	5 + 7	6 + 8	3 + 5

Grade 2　　　　　　　　　Name _____

(Doubles Plus 2, Review)　　　　　　　　　　　Score _____ / 20

You have 2 minutes to complete this assessment.

2 + 4	7 + 5	9 + 9	4 + 6	5 + 5
10 + 9	9 + 7	5 + 3	8 + 6	1 + 9
4 + 6	3 + 7	6 + 6	2 + 9	5 + 7
9 + 8	0 + 6	5 + 2	5 + 4	4 + 4

Grade 2   Name _____

(Make 10 and Extend)   Score _____ / 20

You have 2 minutes to complete this assessment.

| 2 | 8 | 7 | 9 | 3 |
| + 9 | + 5 | + 9 | + 6 | + 9 |

| 6 | 8 | 7 | 5 | 8 |
| + 8 | + 3 | + 5 | + 9 | + 7 |

| 6 | 8 | 7 | 9 | 9 |
| + 7 | + 6 | + 6 | + 5 | + 7 |

| 8 | 6 | 5 | 7 | 8 |
| + 9 | + 5 | + 7 | + 4 | + 5 |

Grade 2   Name _____

(Mixed Review)   Score _____ / 20

You have 2 minutes to complete this assessment.

| 9 | 7 | 8 | 5 | 5 |
| + 4 | + 5 | + 8 | + 6 | + 2 |

| 10 | 9 | 5 | 8 | 1 |
| + 7 | + 7 | + 5 | + 2 | + 9 |

| 4 | 7 | 9 | 2 | 4 |
| + 6 | + 7 | + 6 | + 9 | + 7 |

| 8 | 0 | 6 | 7 | 9 |
| + 8 | + 3 | + 8 | + 6 | + 9 |

Grade 2   Name _____

(Addition and Subtraction Final, Form A)   Score _____ / 40

You have 4 minutes to complete this assessment.

10 − 5	5 + 2	5 − 3	2 + 7	9 − 6
16 − 9	9 + 7	17 − 8	8 + 5	14 − 8
6 − 1	3 + 6	7 − 3	5 + 4	11 − 8
18 − 9	9 + 4	15 − 7	5 + 7	13 − 8
12 − 3	5 + 4	4 − 2	6 + 1	8 − 7
14 − 7	9 + 9	12 − 6	7 + 7	10 − 7
14 − 5	6 + 2	17 − 9	1 + 8	15 − 6
8 − 2	7 + 4	9 − 4	8 + 7	8 − 3

Grade 2   Name _____

(Addition and Subtraction Final, Form B)   Score _____ / 40

You have 4 minutes to complete this assessment.

9 − 6	5 + 2	10 − 5	2 + 7	5 − 3
14 − 8	9 + 7	16 − 9	8 + 5	17 − 8
11 − 8	3 + 6	6 − 1	5 + 4	7 − 3
13 − 8	9 + 4	18 − 9	5 + 7	15 − 7
8 − 7	5 + 4	12 − 3	6 + 1	4 − 2
10 − 5	9 + 9	14 − 7	7 + 7	12 − 6
15 − 6	6 + 2	14 − 5	1 + 8	17 − 9
8 − 3	7 + 4	8 − 2	8 + 7	9 − 4

REFERENCES

Ainsworth, L. (2003). *Power standards: Identifying the standards that matter the most.* Englewood, CO: Lead + Learn Press.

Ainsworth, L. (2010). *Rigorous curriculum design: How to create curricular units of study that align standards, instruction, and assessment.* Englewood, CO: Lead + Learn Press.

Ainsworth, L., & Christinson, J. (1998). *Student generated rubrics: An assessment model to help all students succeed.* Lebanon, IN: Dale Seymour Publications.

Ainsworth, L., & Christinson, J. (2006). *Five easy steps to a balanced math program for secondary grades.* Englewood, CO: Lead + Learn Press.

Ben-Hur, M. (2006). *Concept-rich mathematics instruction: Building a strong foundation for reasoning and problem solving.* Alexandria, VA: ASCD.

Dewey, J. (1933). *How we think.* New York, NY: D. C. Heath & Co.

Harel, G. (2007). The DNR system as a conceptual framework for curriculum development and instruction. In R. Lesh, J. Kaput, & E. Hamilton (Eds.), *Foundations for the future in mathematics education.* Hillsdale, NJ: Erlbaum.

Hattie, J. (2012). *Visible learning for teachers: Maximizing impact on learning.* New York: Routledge.

Hiebert, J., Carpenter, T. P., Fennema, E., Fuson, K., Wearne, D., Murray, H., Oliver, A., & Human, P. (1997). *Making sense: Teaching and learning mathematics with understanding.* Portsmouth, NH: Heinemann.

Kling, G. (2011, September). Fluency with basic addition. *Teaching Children Mathematics 18*(2), *80–88.*

Lobato, J. E., Ellis, A. B., Charles, R. I., & Zbiek, R. M. (2010). *Developing essential understanding of ratios, proportions and proportional reasoning for teaching mathematics: Grades 6–8.* Reston, VA: National Council of Teachers of Mathematics.

Ma, L. (1999). *Knowing and teaching elementary mathematics: Teachers' understanding of fundamental mathematics in China and the United States.* Mahwah, NJ: Lawrence Erlbaum Associates.

Maletsky, E. M., Andrews, A. G., Bennett, J. M., Burton, G. M., Luckie, L. A., McLeod, J. C., Newman, V., Roby, T., and Scheer, J. K. (2004). *Harcourt math.* New York, NY: Harcourt.

Marzano, R. J. (2004). *Building background knowledge for academic achievement.* Alexandria, VA: ASCD.

Marzano, R. J., Pickering, D. J., & Pollock, J. E. (2012). *Classroom instruction that works: Research-based strategies for increasing student achievement* (2nd ed.). Alexandria, VA: ASCD.

Medina, J. (2008). *Brain rules: 12 principles for surviving and thriving at work, home, and school.* Seattle, WA: Pear Press.

National Center for Education Statistics. (2011). *Trends in international mathematics and science study*. http://nces.ed.gov/Timss/

National Governors Association Center for Best Practices & Council of Chief State School Officers. (2010). *Common core state standards for mathematics*. Washington, DC: Authors.

National Research Council. (2001). *Adding it up: Helping children learn mathematics*. J. Kilpatrick, J. Swafford, & B. Findell (Eds.). Mathematics Learning Study Committee, Center for Education, Division of Behavioral and Social Sciences and Education. Washington, DC: National Academy Press.

O'Connell, S., & SanGiovanni, J. (2011a). *Mastering the basic math facts in addition and subtraction: Strategies, activities, and interventions to move students beyond memorization*. Portsmouth, NH: Heinemann.

O'Connell, S., & SanGiovanni, J. (2011b). *Mastering the basic math facts in multiplication and division: Strategies, activities, and interventions to move students beyond memorization*. Portsmouth, NH: Heinemann.

Polya, G. (1945). *How to solve it: A new aspect of mathematical method*. Princeton, NJ: Princeton University Press.

Popham, W. J. (2003). *Test better, teach better: The instructional role of assessment*. Alexandria, VA: ASCD.

Rasmussen, C., Heck, D. J., Tarr, J. E., Knuth, E., White, D. Y., Lambdin, D. V., . . . , Barnes, D. (2011, May). Trends and issues in high school mathematics: Research insights and needs. *Journal for Research in Mathematics Education, 42*(3), 204–219.

Shumway, J. F. (2011). *Number sense routines: Building numerical literacy every day in grades K–3*. Portland, ME: Stenhouse.

Stenmark, J. K., Thompson, V., & Cossey, R. (1986). *Family math*. Berkeley, CA: Lawrence Hall of Science.

Stevenson, H. W., & Stigler, J. W. (1992). *The learning gap*. New York: Touchstone.

Van de Walle, J. A., Karp, K. S., & Bay-Williams, J. M. (2010). *Elementary and middle school mathematics: Teaching developmentally*. Boston, MA: Pearson.

Van de Walle, J. A., & Lovin, L. H. (2005a). *Teaching student-centered mathematics: Grades K–3*. Boston, MA: Pearson.

Van de Walle, J. A., & Lovin, L. H. (2005b). *Teaching student-centered mathematics: Grades 3–5*. Boston, MA: Pearson.

Van de Walle, J. A., & Lovin, L. H. (2005c). *Teaching student-centered mathematics: Grades 5–8*. Boston, MA: Pearson.

Wiggins, G., & McTighe, J. (2005). *Understanding by design* (expanded 2nd ed.). Alexandria, VA: ASCD.

INDEX